UNDERSTANDING THE COMPLEX REALITY OF THE
SCHOOL BUS DRIVER'S JOB

Roman Blaise

 page vision

228 Hamilton Ave.,
Palo Alto, CA 94301

CONTENTS

List Of Abbreviations 5

Introduction...9

Chapter I   A Daily Routine 15

Chapter II   The First Week.................................22

Chapter III   Dealing With A Child.............................27

Chapter IV   Problems Encountered 30

Chapter V   The Longue Journey: True Reality
                   Of A Run Or The Story Of Each Stop 46

Chapter VI   Problems With Parents.............................57

Chapter VII   The Driver's Responsibility When Driving
                   A School Bus...68

Chapter VIII   Hazards Or Distractions Of The Roads...............70

Chapter IX   The Reasons Of Their Acts.........................77

Chapter X   Problems With Other Drivers 80

Chapter XI   Theory And Practice 84

Chapter XII   Harassment On The Road.............................94

Chapter XIII   The Surprises On The Road 98

Chapter XIV   Fear While Working 104

Chapter XV   Being A Substitute Or A Spare Driver 108

Chapter XVI   Effects Of The School Bus On Our Health 117

Chapter XVII   Words I Have Heard 125

Chapter XVIII   Bad Words And Expressions

                 Of Sexual Contents 135

Chapter XIX   Racial Discrimination.......................................141

Chapter XX   Things And People I Have Seen 147

Chapter XXI   One Million Eyes Are Watching Us....................162

Chapter XXII   Incidents And Accidents On The Road 168

Chapter XXIII   Purpose Of The Child Synovial System

                 Or Child Safety System Or Child Alert System.... 178

Chapter XXIV   Observation Of A Sudden Change

                 Of Work Conditions 180

Chapter XXV   The Birth Of The Union....................................189

Chapter XXVI   In Search Of Happiness......................................192

Chapter XXVII   Antwann Joseph 195

Chapter XXVIII   Relation Bus Driver-Students 203

Chapter XXIX   A Clear Conscience 218

Chapter XXX   In The Middle Of The Ocean 227

Chapter XXXI   The Last School Day..236

LIST OF ABBREVIATIONS

1. CFR Court of Federal Regulations
2. 49 CFR Federal Motor Carrier Safety Regulations
3. FMCSA Federal Motor Carrier Safety Administration
4. NYCRR New York Code, Rules and Regulations
5. 8NYCRR New York State Education Department Regulations
6. 17NYCRR New York State Department of Transportation Regulations
7. NHTSA National Highway Traffic Safety Administration

In memory of my great grandmother,
Sylia Christophe.

INTRODUCTION

Two days before the September 11, 2001 disaster, I moved to America with the aim of answering some pertinent questions that life asks. What a terrible way to start a journey in a foreign country! Four airplanes were hijacked, and as a result, thousands of people lost their lives through those attacks.

Seven days after I came here, my father died after suffering from a disease for a long time. I salute or admire the strength and the courage of my father, and to the families of thousands of people who disappeared in such a tragedy, my sincere condolences. May God Almighty continue to give them the strength they need to keep going until they get rid of their sorrow.

Seven years ago, I obtained my Commercial Driver License (CDL). On my first workday, many things have immediately caught my attention, and I started observing every little detail around me while on the job. Therefore, I feel the necessity to share what I witnessed with all of you: the real-life stories and the heartbreaking moments of emotions I have lived while driving. That way, I want to change people's prospective of the reality of the school bus driver's job and unfold the complexity of a job that may seem "easy" on the surface to so many.

To the parents whose children will have to ride the bus to school one day, the reality inside it is different from the fun bus we see on television or in books. The atmosphere inside could be altogether a fun or a nightmare for our children, depending on the drivers' composure and also depending on the children's behavior. It could be fun and ideal, or disarray, distress and displeasure contrary to the children's general impression before they begin to ride the bus. If only all school bus drivers could bring themselves to the level of those kids and empathize with them; if only each and every school bus driver could be caring, patient, responsible, protective, and conscientious or just be human to the children, they would make huge difference in their lives. Our children could be in the nicest bus if they are around children who have been exposed to all the good qualities, virtues, and attributes that characterize the ideal family.

On the contrary, if our children ride a school bus driven by a villain and mean driver, if our children are around bullies, who would tease them and use all kinds of words to belittle or demean them and make them lose their self-worth, the experience on the school bus would be hell on earth. Some of the bullies can go to the point of hitting or harassing them. The victims sometimes cry their eyes out, and their faces would translate all the pains and sufferings they have been through.

Under such circumstances, some drivers will quickly intervene to battle the bullies. Unfortunately, some others would ignore what is going on. As parents, it is our duty to focus our attention on our children and act quickly to prevent any sad event when they are riding a school bus where the driver does not give them any protection whatsoever.

This book is a candid confession. We, as school bus drivers, should not betray our students. Our mission calls us to serve them, to protect them, to drive them safely to school. It is also a denunciation against a very few irresponsible school bus drivers out there who are hypocrite, uncaring, inhuman, and negligent. I am talking about those who sometimes drive while intoxicated by drugs and alcohol; those who never smile; least, those who pay a smile to our children only when they receive the Christmas envelope. This book also denounces the drivers who put an insurmountable wall between them and the students—those the children hate because they have only given them hatred and contempt. I am not living for them.

Nevertheless, I am living for the school bus drivers who have done the best of themselves to put the children in a comfortable and hospitable atmosphere and treat them fairly regardless of their size, origin, color, or sexual orientation.

Today I am writing about the children I have observed throughout my career as a school bus driver. I am writing for the orphan, the poor, the rich, the one who does not find comfort at home, and the ill-favored by nature. I am working with those called *normal* and those called *abnormal* or *students with special needs* with the same professionalism that this job requires. Even when, in some circumstances, I feel my heart tearing apart, I manage myself to keep my composure in order to give them confidence. I also open my arms to the parents, to the officials of the educational system, to my coworkers, to my boss, and to the American people to show them that the only motivation that guides and helps me in this job is love.

I am doing the first step, although some people may disagree with what is being said in this book. Many other educational professionals may have a totally different point of view. Why not? Disagreement, difference, and controversy are all part of life and make of it a challenge.

I am also talking for school bus drivers who do not want to talk about some dramatic events, some chilling or exciting moments they have lived while doing this job; I am voicing the concerns of those who are too shy or too scared to talk.

I do sympathize with the ones who have had some painful experiences that, until now, cannot escape from their memories; I am talking for the ones who have been "hanged or fired", as a coworker used to say, for doing any minor mistake among many people who have done mistakes, and finally those who have been dismissed, sued, condemned after acting rudely with any child or any parent, or after being involved in a preventable accident.

A special thought for the sick and also for the ones who, after the result of a medical report has revealed any unfit illness for the job, were asked to just stop driving and wait somewhere while they were on duty; a requiem for a Haitian brother who died on the job.

We have to bear in mind that school bus drivers are neither devils nor saints. Like all of us, they are human beings capable of doing good and capable of making mistakes.

If it was allowed to influence people's conception of this book, I would say: It is the testimony of an immigrant Haitian. The daily experience on the job has purged my heart and lets all the events in it to drip to create a lake. Any bus driver who bends to look at this deep lake will see the reflection of his face.

The Complex Reality of the SCHOOL BUS DRIVER'S JOB relates to our worries, our fears, our questions, our prejudices, our suggestions, and our souvenirs. In fact, this book tests the driver's patience and honesty; it is a long learning process, a desire of good for the students and a desire to better understand them; it reflects a positive attitude, a thirst of justice for everyone, a surge of fraternity, and a pursuit of happiness. This book is a cry of alarm against bullies and all kinds of verbal, mental, physical, or psychological abuses perpetrated on the bus; a cry of the heart against indifference, prejudice, and bad faith. It answers questions that go in people's minds, questions the system of things, and is waiting for answers. Problems, defense, safety, hypocrisy, prejudice, remorse, fight, despise, communication, solitude, nostalgia, honesty are, among others, many words that characterize this complex job.

This book is a symbiosis or a disagreement. It is the true story of a school bus run that starts from the first stop to the last one, passes and lets behind it the parents' love and sense of sacrifice for their children, the students' trust and indifference toward their driver, the driver's defense on the roads against other drivers, and ends up in the school. This is the story of a school year that begins with the parents' doubts, fear, and questions and culminates with the sobs of a black boy who misses a white female teacher.

Finally, *The Reality of the SCHOOL BUS DRIVER'S JOB* represents drumrolls that give a dance that gathers students, teachers, parents, officials, managers, drivers, etc., on the loving shadow of the American stage, where they liberate themselves from all constraints, problems, differences, resentment to work for the children's well—being and later enjoy and benefit their success in life. The children are the lungs of this sweet America; without them, it cannot breathe. These are the testimonies of the wonderful and sinister moments I have experienced on the bus. Dear reader, you will not want to put this book back, so it is captivating and contagious.

ACKNOWLEDGMENT

Thank God for giving me the strength to work every day, the courage to speak when it is necessary, the wisdom to calm me down when facing tense challenges, and the intelligence to understand confused situations.

Thanks to my great-grandmother who has built my character, to my wife and children who have given me their support, to my little daughter that I have deserted so many mornings in order to go to the quiet parking lot of High School West to develop my ideas, and also to my niece who was the first one to read a portion of the book and gave me her advice.

Thanks to the boss who has invested his life to build this business and to help me support my family, to the management, and to all my coworkers.

Thanks to the police for watching me on the roads and for enforcing the law when it was necessary.

Thanks to the world for their solidarity and their help in the unprecedented earthquake disaster that has destroyed my dear country Haiti.

A special thanks to my friends Jocelyne Rivière, Joliette Jean, Jean Généus, Jhonny Gracia, and Hubert Sharpe for their invaluable support and hard work in helping me write this book.

CHAPTER I

A Daily Routine

At 5:00 a.m., the alarm of the cell phone pierces the silence of the cold morning. I wake up and jump out of bed. First, as a soldier, I bathe and get dressed quickly. I pick up the lunchbox from the refrigerator, and then rush to my car to go to work. Going down on Pulaski Road, I pass by a strong and energetic jogger climbing the hill; and then a few feet away I stop to pick up Jose, my Latino friend who usually rides to work with me. As soon as I get to the company yard, I rush to my school bus to begin to work.

As usual, I do the pretrip inspection as a safety requirement for all bus drivers before any school bus leaves the yard. I walk around the bus to verify if all the exterior elements, such as lights, windshield, emergency doors, tires, are in working condition. Then I go inside the bus to make sure that all the interior components—windows, emergency kits, heaters, fans, dome lights, fire extinguishers, etc.—are working.

Afterward, I warm up the bus for a few minutes. Before leaving the yard, it is a must to check brakes and to make sure that the horns are working properly. I go to the office, stop a few minutes there to greet my coworkers before I begin the run. Quickly, I get a cup coffee and mix it with some cold water to cool it off, and then I swallow it. It keeps me awake and focused on my driving; it also stimulates my body and lifts up my spirit for the morning.

At 6:18 a.m., I begin my route. On my way out of the yard, I make the sign of the cross three times, symbol of my faith, base of my hope. Then I said, "God, I hold the steering wheel, but you are in command. Please watch over me and the children for the day."

Coming out of the yard, I move the bus slowly, the driveway being at the bottom of a hill. I turn right cautiously on Old Northport Road and make a left onto Townline Road. Full of energy, I pass all the schools on Town line Road, cross over Jericho Turnpike, and continue on Commack Road until I reach my first pickup, which is located on a street off Dix Highway.

At this point, the high school run begins.

i. The High School

Every day, I always try to be on time at 6:33 a.m. sharp to pick up the high school students. Sometimes, I can be late due to circumstances beyond my control such as heavy traffic, mechanical malfunction, weather conditions, etc. Bus drivers are required by law to follow the strict rules and regulations in respect with the school bus safety. In addition, we want to set a good example for our students to follow.

At this stop, I pick up more than one student and make it a duty to greet all of them with a smiling face and a heartfelt "Good morning." Some usually respond to my greeting, others don't. Strangely, a few students that I will have to drive throughout the school year will never remember my face.

I continue the first run to the last stop until I pick up all the students. Finally, I proceed to the school. During the run, I also ensure that the aisle of the bus is accessible and clear of any objects. In the fall season, when it is really dark in the morning, I turn the dome lights on, so the students can see while boarding the bus. On my way to the school, they engage in different activities such as eating, or any other tasks.

No eating on the bus! I have learned that in the refreshers, in the meetings, in the pre-entrance class. I have seen this sign in so many buses. In fact, it is not in my habit to prevent the students from eating on the bus. Why? There are things, or some legitimate rights, that we cannot stop children from doing. Don't we eat on the bus, and yet according to 8NYCRR 156.3e5, we school bus drivers are not allowed to eat on the bus? Should we bother ourselves in preventing students from eating instead of fulfilling our daily mission safely and surely? That is why after a trip, regardless of how many times we tell them not to eat, we will eventually find on the bus some leftovers, candy wraps, chips, etc.

I head to High School West with a full warm bus; it moves smoothly through the garden of Dix Hills. In general, in the morning, these students, to fortify their brain, start the day eating breakfast on the bus. They eat snacks, candies, sandwiches, cereals, fruits, etc. When a little breeze goes through the windows or through the latches of the bus, it carries either the smell of the food or the suave and pleasant odor of cologne.

The bus passes through the cold air between the trees. I raise my head to look at the dome mirror; I give a quick glance with my eyes to explore all the corners of the bus. Some students have their faces pale, while others are still sleeping after waking up too early. They might have stayed up late last night either watching an interesting show or a game on television, or doing homework or working on a project. Regardless of all that, my primary responsibility is to make sure I drive them safely to school.

These teenagers sit right behind me because they have to go to school. They have to trust me because the system asks them or forces them to trust me as their bus driver. Therefore, in return, I commit myself to be clear with my conscience. As a bus driver, I have to be sincere with myself. Sincerity in the sense that anytime I take the responsibility to drive a school bus, I should have a very low concentration of alcohol in my blood (BAC less than .04), and no drug in my blood system (NYS Laws and Regulations, 2011, p.58).

If, for instance, I drink the night before, the best thing to do would be to stay home; but staying home for not a good reason means—even if I would get pay—I have a problem with myself. Therefore, as a school bus driver's rule, the best thing is to stay away from alcohol twenty-four hours before driving those children to school. Isn't that crystal clear?

Forty-three students sit quietly behind me. Each one is involved in a particular hobby for the moment: One boy quickly eats a sandwich, some try to take a morning nap, and others are texting as if it is a way of life for them. Others take the opportunity to court a girl, others to kiss, or even to touch each other.

I go down Wolf Hill Road. I look at the clock on top of my head; it is 7:00 a.m. I listen to the morning news from a radio station. Since it is the first school day, I can feel the fever and the excitement on Wolf Hill Road. The westbound traffic to the school forces me to slow down. I enter the school, turn on the dome lights so the students can see; I also turn on the amber lights to warn all drivers around that I am about to stop. I give the right of way to this teacher who is waiting impatiently, then I move right to enter the school ground. I wave to the security guard, move on, and park alongside the curb to drop the students off.

I stop and pull the emergency brake to secure the bus. Using my left hand, I turn the switch to open the door so the children can leave. Some say thanks, while some others don't even look at me.

After all the students get off the school bus, I walk back in the aisle not only in search of sleeping children, but also to clear the bus of a few items such as pens, pencils, books, notebooks, porn magazines, backpacks, matches, cigarettes, money, condoms, knives, morning pills, drugs, and many other surprising items.

Out of High School West, I begin the middle school right after because there is no real free time between the high school run and the middle school run.

ii. The Middle School

Right away, I begin the middle school run. The first pickup time is 7:15 a.m.

The middle school students are usually troublemakers, although that year, I ride some of the best middle school students I ever had. Generally, we spend less time to pick up the students who are waiting at the corner stop than the ones who are waiting for the bus inside their houses. The first ones stay outside three to five minutes until the bus comes, whereas others and the ones who have house stop or live across from the stop, wait inside because the bus must stop and consequently would not miss them. Their parents require them to wait inside due to some legitimate reasons like cold weather, child offenders, impatient drivers, too old, or physically disabled babysitters.

Generally in the morning, school bus drivers do not face too much pressure from parents concerning the loading of the students.

After picking up all the stops, I continue on my way until I drop them off at the middle school, then I post-trip the bus.

Some mornings, during the daily break after the middle school run, I decide to chat with others drivers who meet on one bus or in the school's cafeteria. Some other days, I do personal things like praying, reading a paper or a book, or writing. Usually, I take this opportunity to enjoy my breakfast. If the next pickup is far from the middle school, I go to a place close to the next first stop, so I could be on time in case of heavy traffic or if the road conditions are not ideal.

Around 8:30 a.m., the break is over. I begin to do the elementary school pickups. Those children are the small ones, the most fragile and sensitive.

iii. The Elementary School

Elementary students are the ones who require more attention because they are very little kids. Some schools establish in each bus a safety team where the older ones have to watch the youngest ones. We must admit that even some students who are members of the safety team cause also trouble inside the bus. We agree that children are not born untidy and wild. They become that way due to exterior influence, indifference of parents, excessive abuse, and many other factors that can change their good side.

In the school bus, the little ones, the kindergarteners, sit usually in the first row, right behind me. For being small, they require closer attention; and I have to watch and protect them against the bullying, the teasing, the abuse, and the harassment by kids older than them.

In the morning, very often the parents accompany the elementary students to the bus. On my first school day, one child looked at me, waved his hand, said hi, and then entered. Another little girl was scared and started to cry. I tried to say hello to her and say some words of encouragement to convince her to come on the bus. Against her will, with her frail legs, she climbed the stairs, her right hand on her face. She was probably shy or capricious and did not want to look at me, a stranger. Isn't she a girl? Even at a tender age, capriciousness is the prototype of the female gender.

Very often, the elementary children behave in the morning run. Experience has taught me that the complications are mostly in the afternoon run.

After picking up all the students, I head to the elementary school with a full bus, whose content averages sixty-one naïve and innocent students, sixty-one passengers and witnesses of my every move. These students are so different from the others ones—they are not sleeping but awake and alert to observe the least details. They question me, want to know my name, report my behavior to their parents and teachers, judge and even influence, in many cases, some decisions of the high-ranked school officials. This run is what I call the "feeling of the job." It is a feeling that hurts when they begin to run in the aisle, a feeling where we feel what we are getting paid for.

Now our mind does not have to watch only the roads, we also have to watch the children whose behavior represents a kind of distraction that can contribute to any accident during a trip. According to the Table 7(P) of the NYSDMV, 21.6 percent of school vehicles accidents were caused by driver's distraction, and 0.4 percent by passenger's distraction.

Driving a school bus is a challenging job. Anytime the bus is moving, no one is allowed to stand up, walk in the aisle, jump on the seats, or behave in a way that can either disturb and distract the bus driver or jeopardize the safety of anyone on the bus. Gently and firmly, a disciplinary code is established at the beginning of the school year in order to permit the students to familiarize, observe, and understand me as a human being partially different from their parents. Even though the ambiance on the bus seems different from the one in their home, we should sometimes shape it in an ideal way: no trouble on the bus.

On the one hand, some of them do misbehave and stop when our eyes meet through the dome mirror; on the other hand, some others do not care even if I am looking at them. They just continue to misbehave. Students who do not listen to me and refuse to follow the rules must be reported. Even some safety team members, whose duty is to control and report the students' behavior on the bus, have not been spared when they cross the limits.

One safety member's parent was mad at me after her daughter has been reported. As if being in a safety team makes this child a privileged, invincible student. Aren't they also children who need to be disciplined? My role is to create an environment where the students feel secured and where I can drive safely to the school.

Courage, discipline, patience, rigor, sense of duty, self-respect, and so on are the qualities that we need to complete the first portion of the day. Every morning looks like that; some others are more stressful.

The first week is always a crazy week for the bus driver.

CHAPTER II

The First Week

i. The Morning Route

The first week of school is the craziest, the most stressful one for me. As a school bus driver, I have to face all the difficulties of the job, learn all the complexity of the new route, respond to all kinds of questions, comply to some strange orders, deny some impossible favors, challenge certain funny exigencies, and even ignore some threats from a few parents.

Here are some evident cases.

ii. A Skeptical Mother

Any argument between the bus driver and the parents is not permitted. I have to drive innocent, immature, influential witnesses: the students. Indeed, I have to behave myself and act kindly, cautiously, and respectfully; but some days are beyond my control. In fact, the parents, or the exigencies of the moment, force me to argue. Even when it is bad, I have to do it politely.

In September 2007, I argued with a mother the first school day. It was about a stop on a street off Commack Road. The policy of the company prevents its employees to "discuss routes, timing, etc., with parents, school district employees, or any other persons outside the company"(EBI Policy Manual p. 32, sec. 10). That morning, this skeptical mother, for safety reasons, wanted to know if I would have to go on this stop with all the children, including her daughter. Because it was my first morning, I couldn't catch the meaning of her request. I felt a little confused. Then she asked me while extending her right hand toward me. "Let me see the papers."

"No, madam," I replied, shaking my head negatively. I added, "The lefts and rights are private to the company. I don't have to show you anything. If you need more information, call the district. Sorry I have to leave." I closed the doors and continued on.

iii. Wrong Conception

On that first school day, I went inside a court shaped as a number nine. According to the lefts and rights, I had to pick up at the stops provided by the school district. I stopped at number 3333 to wait for a child. The mother at the next house (a distance of five feet between the two driveways) ordered me to pick up her son in front of her house, although he belonged to the previous stop. That mother's order conflicted with the number eleven of the general driver instructions: "Do not accept any instructions regarding changes, pick-ups or drop-offs from ANYONE other than your dispatcher or safety department" (EBI Policy Manual, p. 32 sec. 11).

Through my right mirrors, I watched her walking along the bus and stop by the door. Menacingly, she told me, "Why didn't you pick up my son in front of my house?"

I replied, "I'm sorry, ma'am. I didn't have this number in my chart."

"Why do you stop in front of her house when you cannot stop in front of mine?"

With a smile I added, "It's not like that. I have to follow the left and right sheets."

Firmly, she commanded me, "Tomorrow, I want you to pick up my son in front of my house."

"Yes, ma'am! I don't have any problem picking up your son in front of your house. Why not! I'm a soldier ready to serve. Just call the district and they will order me. Sorry I have to leave."

I closed the door and left.

iv. The Caring Dad

I closed the doors, and clockwise, my eyes scanned carefully the seven mirrors, and at the same time, my head moved and drew an imaginary pentagon to make sure it was safe to leave. I went to the next stop, ignoring what would be the next order. At the stop, a father accompanied three children to the bus. He helped the youngest one to climb the stairs, and then he looked at me and gently introduced himself. "I'm John. What's your name?"

Being a Creole- and French-speaking person, I always have difficulty to pronounce Roman in English, so I responded, "Roman, like the Roman Empire."

He came near the doors; politely, he joined his hands then added, "Could you tell me the pickup time?"

"Well, it's a little difficult to give you a time. It's only the first school day," I replied.

"The school district asked us to be out at 8:51 a.m. Are you going to be here at this time?

"To be clear, I can't give you a time yet. The only sure thing is my first pickup is at 8:35 a.m. Next week I'll give you the right time."

"OK."

v. The Afternoon Route

After the morning route, if I do not have midday, the company gives me the choice to bring the bus home as long as I do not park it in the street. If I have midday, I drive the bus back to the yard and wait at the office until it is time to begin the afternoon route. During my first months on the job, I have confronted some stressful and unforgettable moments.

In fact, if I stay home for the midday to relax or to rest, I will be fine to do the afternoon run. Otherwise, if I do a midday, I then eat lunch before beginning the afternoon run; I have the impression that a Dambala Kò likid invades my body as the famous Haitian comedian Rene Depestre said. Indeed, it is a transformation, which crosses the body and puts it in a graceful state. At that time, I have to control myself in order to stay focused to direct the bus.

In case I have a short break after the morning run, I take the opportunity to sweep the bus. However, if I don't have time in the morning, when I get to the high school in the afternoon, I sweep the floor, open the doors and emergency exit to change the air inside. I clean the mirrors, buckle the seatbelts, and wipe the dashboard—this part of the bus that gives the parents the first impression of who I am. Furthermore, since I spend all day on the bus, I have to keep the environment clean so that the students and I can breathe freely and are away from any contamination.

It is 2:10 p.m., the time to begin to drop off the students. When I leave the high school, most of the students often sit down immediately or later; others will sit until I ask them to do so, or will need me to either convince or force them to sit down. A few of them will not listen to me. I have the choice either to let them stand up or to keep asking them to sit down and proceed to their destinations.

Being new on the job, I get easily angry at them; I order them to sit down using a strong tone voice. But after a year on the job, I understood it was better to approach them, speak gentle to them, and explain to them why they have to sit down. I feel deeply sorry for the ones I used to scream at due to the circumstances of the moment.

After completing the run, I head to the middle school.

The middle school students could sometimes be a real headache. For example, during my first year, one of the boys I drove was very rebellious and also very funny. He often joked using a funny and dirty language. The girls adored him and liked his company. I had to report him twice for misbehaving.

Some of those kids gave me my first baptism of fire. Some days, I had to pull over many times to talk to them and explain to them the safety rules. I tried to be fair to them, but sometimes I was even forced to yell in order to make them sit down. I have reported many of them. In the worst cases, I even had to ask for the principal or other school officials for assistance. Being teenagers, I think at this age, they were probably going to another phase of their lives.

How students from the elementary school behave? The elementary school students are the youngest, but they are also troublemakers.

In general, students who ride large bus do not have to keep their seatbelts on (NYS Laws and Regulations, 2011, p. 104). Therefore, this law sets them free to create all kinds of trouble for the school bus drivers.

The first school day, some parents advise or force their kindergarteners to wear their seatbelts. They would keep it on only for a few days until a first or second grader teases them, or convinces them that it is not necessary. Elementary students are the ones who give all kinds of problems such as switching seats, fighting, pushing, and teasing. Since they sometimes cause real distractions, we need to be focused and use the maximum attention to drive them safe to destination.

CHAPTER III

Dealing With A Child

Before giving any more details, let me explain to you my experience with my first daughter. I am in the category of people who have to raise a child without planning. Yes, I raised my first daughter as an inexperienced father. It took me time to understand her behavior. Consequently, for not being ready and prepared, there were times I yelled at her and forced her to do things against her will. Some mornings, before she went to preschool, I used to force her to eat early. Eventually, she would vomit each time. Finally, I realized that her system would not tolerate food in the morning. This is only a way to tell you that being a bus driver requires some training and experience with children.

I do believe that in the school system, the students' well-being, their education, their training, and their protection represent the center of interest of every adult interacting with them. In fact, we need to have a big heart to deal with children. I know some bus drivers who never have experience with children; some others never have children; others decide not to have for their own reason; and worst, there are the ones who cannot conceive any child. Depending on the way we face problems caused by the children, we could be blamed, kick out of the run, or simply fired.

In Candlewood Middle School, one driver showed me his card and said, "I'm a retired police officer. I don't play with children. I will treat them like little soldiers. Either you follow the rules or you are out of the bus."

Who do you think was out the next week? The bus driver.

Dealing with students requires tact, dexterity, patience, rigor, and suppleness. If we are too rigid the system just breaks us.

i. Hurry of Inexperience

"An experienced person is a prophet," said a Jamaican coworker. In other words, he can see the other side of the wall. To the novice school bus driver, children are little angels; their words and comments should be carefully listened. Let me explain a strange and important lesson I have learned the first school day after mistakenly managing the bus.

In September 7 2004, my first day as a big bus driver, I began the elementary run at 8:25 a.m. I stopped in Astro Place, Dix Hills; the first student who entered the bus was a girl. Then I picked up students from the second stop, the third, the fourth, etc.

At some stops, to retain a memory of that day, the parents took pictures of the students. They also took my picture as a souvenir but also for the record. While the students were getting on the bus and it began to fill up with people, I became more nervous. Given that I was running out of time, I began to rush. This is the worst thing to do when driving a bus. One thing to remember was that I had children on board, not boxes. That morning, the bus was full of innocent people, precious packages, wonderful creatures, the future of America, and the most beautiful gifts their parents ever have.

It was not my first day as a school bus driver, though I was nervous because it was my first day driving a large bus full of children. What circumstances stopped me to rush that day? What forced me to slow down? What made me regain control of myself and, as a matter of fact, regain control of the situation inside the bus?

It was a student. It was a child, a girl, a wonderful girl. Thank you! That day, she got on the bus and was walking to her assigned seat. I released the brakes in order to move. While she was walking in the aisle, I ordered her, "Sit down! Sit down! Find a seat."

She responded politely, "I've never seen a bus driver like that!"

This innocent sentence entered my ears, crossed all my body, and went through me like an arrow. Right away, out of good conscience, I started to slow down, then stopped, and let her sit down. The rule is, "Do not move the bus when someone is walking in the aisle." In case of injury, I will be accounted for and probably sued. The famous verb to sue is one of the most conjugated in America.

I was not aware that the school district gives drivers an interval of fifteen minutes after the entrance time. I got this information many months later. So anytime in the hurry of inexperience, any child or any subordinate can teach us some salutary principles.

I continued the run with the elementary students. They were the troublemakers; some were among the worst during the first day of school. School bus drivers, get ready to face all kinds of problems throughout the route.

CHAPTER IV

Problems Encountered

i. Problems with Students

In September 2004, more than forty-eight children were sitting behind me. With a stony accent, I talked to them, and some days I was forced to yell in order to cover forty to fifty children's voice. In fact, the first month I had to shape them my way, the way the system wanted it.

Anyone who is reading this portion might ask this question, "Why didn't you talk to them, give them your system, explain to them what you want or what you don't?" Sure I did that, but not in the first trip.

During the first trip to the elementary school, the students on the bus were in a fever of anticipation: cry, nostalgia, excitement, joy. This little girl with misty eyes missed mom. For at least six hours, perhaps for the first time, she was not going to see her. Now she felt sad for being part of a strange world. It was her first day to school.

That third grader boy was jumping of excitement. This boy and the other students were happy because they were going to meet their friends. They could not wait to show their friends their new clothes, new books, new backpacks. It was the same excitement we had when we were students. A little curious and nervous to meet their new teachers, they were thinking about the new classes, the challenges, the new programs, and the new experiences. There were so many reasons that translated their excitement and could all of a sudden change their behavior on the bus.

To the nostalgic girl, I said, "Are you OK?"

She acquiesced by shaking her head and then shyly responded, "Yes."

Eventually, a bigger one would talk to her and comfort her. Actually, it was her first day. I just had to create an ideal environment so that she got along with me, the bus driver.

Other students started to fight, to spit on each other, walk in the aisle, tease other students, or engage in activities that angered me sometimes. Obviously, I would have to report them in different occasions when it was necessary. Reporting is part of the job. It is a part of the process of discipline, part of the code of conduct. Nevertheless, we should report with tact and for a good and evident reason. We should not let ourselves get trapped in cycle of reports that would give the management, the parents, and the district a false impression of ourselves. Remember, they are children. We should also try to be as patient as we can.

ii. Code of Conduct

All bus drivers have their own code of conduct, their own way of disciplining. Some are more efficient than others. I have to establish my own system so that the students get adjusted to it as long as it does not conflict with the rules and regulations.

Driving a bus is a choice. It is also an interesting job. It could be fun as well as a tough challenge.

To face this challenge, I like my home system: We don't wait until it's too late to discipline a child; we have to begin at an early age. We do it while the child is young. In fact, we, as bus drivers, do it the first school day. Education begins at the crib (French proverb). Do not interpret this as an abuse: A child gets its first spank at an early age. Most of the time, if we wait too long, either we would have to beat or correct him when he becomes a dangerous adult for the society, or he would be the one to beat or murder us.

It would be better to discipline them. As William E. Homan expresses in an article of The Art of Living, "Discipline is important because we live in an organized society where, if you have not learned life's requirements at an early age, you will be taught them later, not by those who love tempers the lesson but by strangers who couldn't care less about the harm they do to your personality"(Reader's Digest, 1969).

I cannot recall even once being spanked by my great-grandmother. Though anytime we made eye contact, I immediately understood her. I use the same principle on my bus. Therefore, a simple look through the mirror translates my intentions to the students. That is why most of the time, any child at fault would quickly sit down once our eyes meet. To be clear, children on my bus are familiar with the established system, which requires them to sit down while the bus is moving. This is the primary rule on the bus. I do not allow them to stand up during a trip. If the students keep standing, I will pull over to talk to them and explain to them why I want everyone to sit down: question of safety. When driving in a street where it is unsafe to stop, and if the bus is not equipped with microphone, I use the other tool, my voice. I would yell at them to get their attention. I also yell to cover their voices, sixty voices. After three warnings, the next sanction is a simple report.

If the new system is setting up well, even in the case where new stops are added, the new students will not have too much problems to fit in. I rarely will have to yell later. Some of the other children, who know and already agree with my system, will warn and convince them to follow the regulations.

If we do not accept to do it at the beginning of the school year, on many occasions, we will have to pull over, call the principal, and report the students so many times we would become annoying and even ridiculous.

Two direct consequences can result from our lack of discipline. The first one, after so many reports, they might take one child off our bus—a decision which could cause some emotional consequences for this child because he would be isolated from the ambiance and far from his closed friends. The second one the school district, or the company, can decide to simply take the driver off the route.

iii. The Perfect Bus

The idea of an ideal or perfect bus is pure fiction. A way to tell you that some days will be difficult. I have had days when I couldn't control the students. As a result, I had the choice either to finish the run or return to the school. One thing is sure, once they fit into our system, we won't have so many disturbances on our bus. Remember, they are children.

Yes, they are children; they are human beings. We should understand their impulses, their feelings, and their behavior. But the reality inside the bus forces us to act quickly. Indeed, we should act in real time, in the sense that no real dialogue or advice can take place when the bus is moving fast.

People might find it shocking when I say I yell at the children. There were days when I yelled spontaneously. One day, a dispatcher was surprised after I made such a confidence to her. To tell the truth, until I became a bus driver, I never had the habit to yell in my life. An author said, "Yelling is a way to intimidate somebody when you don't feel secure." I remember during my first month in the job, anytime I spoke loud, anytime I yelled, I began to cough. My vocal cords were not used to that. To any large bus driver who never found himself in a situation to yell, I raise my hat out of respect.

Yelling is part of the job. This necessary tool helped us sometimes warn the students immediately instead of waiting for later. In order to save the patient's life, the doctor should stop the flow of blood that is coming out of the vein that has been cut, so he yelled to a distracted nurse. In fact, the primary concern of all school bus drivers is the children's safety and the condition *sine qua non* to guarantee their safety is to drive in an environment that does not distract them from the road. In other words, we should drive in a quiet environment, where some children's behavior would not be tolerated.

Frankly, during some trips, in order to travel safe to the school, I was forced to talk loud, sometimes to yell, and to even scream. Although against our will, we use this tactic to face this challenging task of driving and, at the same time, controlling the bus.

iv. Screaming and its Consequences

In 1987, I visited my friend Jean, who injured his testicles during training in the Haitian Military Academy. We were talking when a sergeant entered the room.

Jean, a tall, heavy built man shouted at the sergeant, "Rompez! (Get out!)"

The scared sergeant ran back out. I was surprised to discover that kind of rude reaction in him. I said, "Why do you have to scream?"

Calmly, he responded, "Roman, it's part of the job. It's something you do automatically. They teach us to scream."

I cannot remember how many times I had to repeat or scream the verb *sit down*. We, school bus drivers, have not been taught how to scream. No instructor, even once, ever urged us to do so during a training session or a refresher, though some bus drivers scream, and the consequences could be disastrous for a child.

A scream can sometimes hurt a kindergartener who eventually would fear to come back on the bus. To illustrate my case, I would tell you of a story of a little girl. One afternoon on my way to the students' homes, I noticed from the dome mirror one little boy and his brother running in the aisle. I saw a disaster coming. In fear, I screamed so loud that the little girl, a kindergartener, who sat behind me jumped from her seat. The next day, her mother had to force her to get on the bus. During the entire trip to the elementary school, she turned her head and looked away from me.

Now, was my reaction a good one? Not really. But it was necessary. It was a choice between two evils. Later, I apologized to that little creature.

We must understand sometimes there are reasons enough for someone to yell. I have also been yelled at by a teacher; the following case shows that.

On September 9, 2010, a teacher in East Northport yelled at me. In fact, she was upset because I entered the Christian school parking lot while the children began to board the buses. Being a spare driver and not aware of the regulations, I pulled in the school's parking lot to pick up the students. The female teacher, wearing a fluorescent rain coat and holding a walkie-talkie, stopped me from entering the parking lot. She shouted, "Turn around and go pick up at the circle located in front of the school."

I moved forward, entered the parking lot's west side that was empty. She followed the bus; I opened the door, and she screamed, "Why did you come in the parking lot? I told you to turn around and go on the circle."

"No bus there. I cannot turn the bus in the middle of the street," I answered.

"I don't care! Go around the block and turn around."

"But the parking lot is empty."

She shouted, "I don't care. Where do you hear?"

I felt my blood pressure skyrocketing and boiling in my veins, but I controlled myself and tried not to start an argument with her. I was not allowed to. And moreover, after exactly nine years in America and almost seven years driving a school bus, I knew how to handle that particular problem. But she noticed that I was not happy about the incident, and she cleared the way to let me proceed to pick up the students. Jesus Christ, pray for me!

Now, let us analyze that little event.

Sincerely, she did not have to know the circumstances that caused me to be late. In fact, the previous school is located in Brookhaven, so it took me more than forty-five minutes to complete the run and come to the Christian school. It was a rainy day (she wore a raincoat); therefore, the road conditions were bad (that was my business); it is not recommended to do a U-turn in the middle of a busy street (it was 2:45 pm; she was not aware of the company's policy). What interests her for the moment was the complete safety of the students. Wasn't she right to scream at me?

Screaming is necessary, and I feel a necessary obligation to apologize toward the students afterward. I approach and explain to them why I have to scream sometimes—requirement of the moment. Not that I am rude or mean. On the contrary, we, as school bus drivers, are in majority fathers and mothers who also have children. Behind the steering wheel, we represent a friend, a brother, a protector. So we understand them.

Thus, as children, they can play quietly as long as they stay in their seats. We should tell and show them that we love them, we believe in them. We should tell them how wonderful they are. We yell not because we want to hurt them, but our basic objective is to discipline and help them improve. They are the future of America. We should explain to them that they would not have to go to jail if they respect the society's rules and conditions. Life would smile at them. We should tell them that now is the time to take the chance that America gives them, not later, not in an uncertain future. We should tell them that, as children, they are the most wonderful people, the most beautiful people in the world.

I like to ask them, "Do you have a dog?" Usually, they'll say yes.

"When you talk to the dog, does he behave?"

"Yes."

"So why we, as human beings, don't want to behave?"

Sometimes I kneel in front of the children when doing this. I have learned this from my cousin who used to jump, roll on the ground, and kneel in front of his four kids. This is an important tool: We kneel and we appear to have the same height as them. I do not want to be taller; I do not want to give them the impression that I need to dominate. Now is not the time to dominate. Now, I am not behind the wheel; we are friends. So let's talk! Let's talk now as good friends, forgetting that the world exists only for me and my students. Let's forget about my frustrations at home.

v. Frustrations at Home

We should not bring our frustrations at home to the school bus. Problems in our family, in life, our bills, our prejudices, our fear, our skeptical questions, our jealousy, and so on should be kept for ourselves. As a matter of fact, a husband died on the bed with his wife sleeping next to him. He did not want to ask for her help because they had an argument the evening before. I, in particular, have a pact with my wife. "Anytime I am on the bed, we are friends." Can we be enemy with our close colleagues? We have to do the job ignoring our differences. The same formula applies on the bus. The students have to interact with us. They sit behind us. Let us be smart. Transform our job as a place of pleasure, a crib of love. Those sitting behind us only have love in their hearts. We yell at a child, we spank him, but he comes right back to us. Don't we have a heart?

Frustrations can cause us to feel angry. We should create for ourselves an environment where our least trace of anger does not materialize. By experience, getting angry behind the wheel gives us the impression that we drive faster than the speed limit. Driving above the speed limit means less safety conditions. So if we are frustrated or angry with our wife, our children, our boss, or another driver on the roads, we should be sure to control ourselves.

Do not forget our primary duty: Drive the children safely to school; therefore, we should leave our frustration at home.

vi. The Intransigent Students

The intransigent students refer to the ones hard to control. I am talking about students whose behavior, at the early age, was not guided or ordered by someone. They naturally like doing something good for themselves, but that is in disagreement with the regulations on the bus. Screaming or yelling would not stop them from disturbing the school bus. Even if we report them, even if we call the principal, they keep creating problems.

Eventually, it is important to try to find some solutions. First, we approach our managers, the school officials, teachers, principals, assistant principals, or parents. It is necessary to report them at least once, or as many times as we can, according to the safety request so that in case of any incident, there is at least a document on file to protect us in court after any eventual lawsuit would have been filed.

Another powerful tool I like to use is isolation. When the bus is not crowded, I isolate the intransigent student. I order the child to move and sit down between two empty rows. In most case, a kindergartener's first reaction would be to cry. But any second grade student, or higher grade who is forced to sit down behind me, would feel ashamed and upset. Basically, elementary students consider sitting in any front row degrading—an implicit way to identify them as kindergarteners.

Strangely, in my experience as a school bus driver, I drove one student who, even after being moved and isolated, found other ways to create problems.

vii. Stressful Situations

This is an important matter; every society has its code of conduct. It remains impossible for a school bus driver to drive and spank the students, but in some situations, it is necessary for parents or even teachers to use force to correct them. For sure, no one, including bus driver and teacher, dares even touch a student; but a student is entitled to hurt another one.

One day, I was shocked to see a boy hitting a little one. In a fraction of minute, the little boy's face became red like a tomato. This harmless boy's reaction was to cry. At that time, I was a driver assistant; I had to simply make him sit away from the aggressor and later on wrote a report. That's it! Justice was done.

A school bus driver should be able to handle stressful situations: argument between students, sporadic disputes, and even some brawls on the bus. We have seen bloody fights: A student has been beaten up on my bus by another student from another route. The little ones would fight for many circumstances. These incidents have happened so many times inside the bus. We found ways to control ourselves and continue to drive without shaking.

My second shock was an observation I have made in a Candlewood middle school. From the driver's seat, I observed how the fear of the system has literally tied the teacher's hands. That afternoon, I witnessed a middle school boy hurting another little one. On top of him, he punched him for almost ten seconds. The other students were yelling, crying, observing this horrible scene from a distance like me. They came to school to learn and be prepared for tomorrow, not to be a witness of unreasonable and bloody fights. The boys did not have the same size.

My shock doubled when I saw a teacher running to the scene and blowing a whistle to catch the attention of the other teachers. Many others joined her and rushed to help her separate the little boy under the bigger one, who did not want to release him until he had achieved his act.

You would say a predator who grabs a little lizard as his prey for the day. We are not predators. That day, I was very upset because that boy thought he had the right to hurt a student; but no one had the right to hurt him, no one could pull a belt to punish him and make sure he will not hurt another child in the future. I have the impression that this precaution manifested by the teachers toward him makes the world become mean when a bigger child can hurt a little one just for the sake of doing it. I think they can beat him back; the law is clear about that.

In fact, the subdivision c of the section 8 NYCRR 19.5a (3)(ii), which prohibits corporal punishment stipulates, "In situation in which alternative procedures and methods not involving the use of physical force cannot reasonably be employed, nothing contained in this section shall be construed to prohibit the use of reasonable physical force for the purpose 'of protecting any pupil…from physical injury.'"

viii. Problems with High and Middle School Students

To tell the truth, in most cases, high school students are the quiet ones. It's really difficult to have problems with them in the morning. I remember one of them from High School East did not want to sit down even in the morning. He was not really a bad like I thought. It takes me time to realize that, for his height, it was difficult for him to sit down because his knees, even bended, couldn't fit between the seats.

In the afternoon, these students are usually standing when I am leaving the school, since they still have the fever of the day. Again, I have to explain to them why they have to sit down. I usually wave at them to remind them to sit down.

Sometimes, they fight, curse, and tease other students, pedestrians, or even other drivers.

Anytime I catch students fighting, I must report them. No chance. I report both of them. I warn any child who curses or uses a dirty language.

Though throughout the years, I understand that cursing, that is to say, the f word, the s word, the b—ch word, the n word, and so on are part of their life, part of the American culture. I even heard a son using these funny words while he was talking to his mother on the phone.

Obviously, it is ridiculous to report a high school student for these ordinary words. After two years, when I began to understand the essence of the American language, I realized that these ordinary curses, these words starting with *f, n, c, s, b,* are not allowed but tolerated. Read this, what would be your reaction if you heard a middle school boy break the tension inside the bus when he said, "F—k me, babe!"

I'm not asking you to make that word part of your vocabulary. Honestly, I had to struggle to keep myself from laughing when I heard it.

ix. A Bizarre Girl

From the day I began to drive a school bus, I have not confronted too much problems with students. The most serious argument occurred on my first year with a high school girl, a bizarre girl.

She would get upset every time a laugh or a word came from a boy. She would confront that boy even when he laughed to himself. I noticed that she had a complex issue. Sometimes she would raise a big argument with the boy and even fought with him. Therefore, she put me in situation where I had to report her.

One day, I was heading south on Bagatelle Road, right after the Long Island Expressway Bridge; she started a violent fight with the boy. I pulled over, and I was trying to explain to her that her attitude inside the bus was reprehensible when she began to threaten me. She was talking very close to my face. Perhaps her intention was to push me, or simply say to me, "What do you want to do with that?"

Evidently, each word let escape tens of droplets of saliva in my face. I asked her for her name, but she categorically refused to give it to me. Let me mention that it was 2005, my first year driving a large bus. Back then, I did not have the experience and the tact to convince her to give me her name. Angry and powerless, I walked to the boy and asked him his name. Without any resistance, he gave me his name. Since it would not be fair to do one report, how can I find that girl's name?

x. Incoherent Discipline

I wanted to finish that case until I found out her name in order to report both students. I explained the situation to the Safety Section; the safety manager told me to put her address in the report. Since I did not have her name, I used her address as reference. This report did not keep her from making trouble on the bus.

One afternoon, I was picking up students in High School East. I saw a teacher; I called him and asked him for the girl's name while she was standing at the curbside. He did not know. I explained to him the reason I needed the name. He said to me, "You know. Don't force her. If she doesn't want to give you her name, go inside the school and ask for her name."

I went inside, and nobody could give me that information. When I realized that it was impossible to find her name, I dropped this case and I murmured, "That's it! I'm not doing this route next year." Then at the end of August 2005, I chose another route during the pick.

Let me clarify something for the reader. Basically in September, school bus drivers are guided, among others, by two principal motives in the choice of a new route: The first one, the area; and the second one, the tips. On one side, the more ideal the area is, the least problems we face(parents or a babysitters are usually waiting for the disabled students or the kindergarteners), the more tips we get. On the other side, I never notice a senior driver who deliberately decides to choose a route in a non-ideal area, because with it are so many problems and responsibilities (Nobody to get the disabled students and the kindergarteners. These ones, after being dropped off, are sometimes running behind the school bus, while others tent to climb behind it). Scary!

Remember, the sword of Damocles is on top of our heads when we know that all the responsibilities will be on the driver's shoulders. If this statement is a lie, may any driver have the courage to deny it. For me, as a spare driver, I have to drive all kinds of students, take up all the challenges, and face all the responsibilities.

The next school year, I picked another route, a better one, whose students were generally quiet and had better behavior. Surprisingly that year, I had to deal with one of the worst high school students I ever had. Although he was easygoing and funny, sometimes he did strange things that crossed the limits.

xi. The Dangerous Student

One afternoon, I was dropping off students in Dix Hills when that boy began to tease me and the students on board. He cursed at one street worker, then took a soda can from the floor and threw it at him. In fact, he put me and the other students on board in a dangerous situation. I pulled over to warn him of his dangerous behavior.

When I got to the school the next morning, I asked dispatch to call the principal to come on the bus in order to warn him. That morning, the principal and two other teachers entered the bus and took him for disciplinary action.

Even after that incident, his behavior did not improve, and he continued to disturb the ride. In the middle of the school year, he stopped riding the bus. One morning, I saw him walking in the school with a lady, perhaps his mother. A few weeks later, another driver gave me the sad news that he has been thrown away from the high school, because that year was his last chance to change his conduct.

Truly, I did not know how serious his case was. Some days, when I was dropping off by his house in the afternoon, I felt my heart tearing apart to see him walking in the street. The bus passed by him, and surprisingly, he would waived at me. No hard feelings! Sometimes his skateboard or his bike raced the school bus until I dropped his brother off. Some other days he stood alone in the street, a bottle of soda in his back pocket and a cigarette in his mouth, his eyes looking at the sky in search of a flock, in search of a protector. He became part of the lost and dangerous children that the system has damaged.

xii. Retaliation of Students

Some students retaliate against the bus driver after being reported or warned. That same school year, a violent student retaliated against me. The list of angry students' reaction is long: spitting on the seats, cutting of the seats, dropping chewing gum on the floor, fastening the seatbelts, graffiti on the seats, sexual drawings and trap in the aisle, and so on.

One day, this boy punched another boy in the face. I warned and later reported him. In the middle of the school year, in March of 2006, he was running in the aisle. With a severe tone of voice, I warned him, "Could you sit down quietly? I don't have to tell you the same thing every day. Are you a kindergartener or are you in high school?" He didn't respond.

A few weeks after a post-trip, I noticed five burn marks in the backseat. No student on the bus could tell me who did it. It was until after he had moved to Florida that his friend told me that he used a lighter to burn the seat: A way to retaliate against my strong warning.

xiii. Adult Students

a) The South Shore Bus

Children do not represent the only troublemakers on the bus. Strangely, adult students, who lack a solid education, act also like children. Adults who are not carefully prepared also cause problems on the bus, sometimes worst than the children.

One scary experience that I confronted with adult students who were riding my bus is unforgettable. It was not an accident; I was not beaten up, and I did not get shot. It was just a pilgrimage and a penitentiary trip.

Four years ago, around 4:15 p.m., I used to do the North Shore shuttle from Wilson Tech to the North Shore. That Wednesday, more students than usual had to go to the South Shore. Because I was driving a large bus, the dispatcher, after an agreement with a teacher, ordered me to switch route with the South Shore driver who had a van. Then by professional ethic, I agreed politely to drive them home, bearing in mind the idea that the trip would be maybe only half an hour or one as usual.

Since it was the autumn season, it quickly became dark around 5:00 p.m. I dropped the first students at Copiague High School, and then two other students helped me find their houses. Now began my punishment. The left and right sheets were not necessary, given that I had to drive adults; they would direct me to their destinations. For the first time, the students did not want to give me directions. That night, I was lost and confused. I tried to ask them, "What's the next stop?"

No answer. No one cares!

They were doing all kinds of unthinkable things on the bus while it was dark outside and inside. Guess the rest. They didn't want to direct me until they had finished what they were doing. Or was it a tactic to have more time to satisfy some urgent needs or some bestial instincts? I spent more than one hour driving around the South Shore.

Being lost I decided to communicate with the base. No answer. Because of the distance, we have a short range radio; I could not get in touch with the dispatcher. Finally, when I realized that I was on Deer Park Road, I entered a secondary street, parked, and secured the bus.

Their irresponsibility angered me. I got off the driver seat and shouted, "Guys, I'm going to drive you back to the school. I can't play game."

Then I went to my seat and decided to make a U-turn. When they realized that I was serious, each one began successively to direct me to their house. During the trip, I didn't talk too much to them; but the only thing I said was, "I feel sad for you guys because you look just like me."

That night, I dropped them off and got to the yard that day at 7:00 p.m. The next day, I went to the dispatcher's office to see Anita, a wonderful, gentle, and easygoing coworker. I told her, "I had a terrible trip last evening."

She responded, "What happened?"

"Last night, those students made my life a living hell. They did not want to give me direction to their houses, and they were doing all kinds of stuff on the bus. Please, I don't want to have this experience anymore."

"OK, I'll notify the school."

Until the end of the year, I never drove those adult kids.

b) My Own Experience

During my life as a student what kind of behavior did I have while inside a vehicle?

1. The *Tap Tap*

I was living in the town of Martesana located in the western part of Port-au-Prince. In the morning, I used to walk two to three miles to school. In the afternoon, my sister and I used to ride the *tap tap*, a traditional Haitian bus or pickup that brought us quickly home. (In Creole, *tap tap* means quickly.)

One afternoon, the *tap tap* was almost empty of its content. Only another passenger, my sister, and I were inside. I was nine years old. As a troublemaker, I sat at the end of the bench in order to observe the people in the street, the pink flamingoes in the shore, and the Gerard Denis's monkeys and to contemplate the panorama of Port-au-Prince. My sister stayed quietly all the way in the front, right behind the window that separates us from the driver.

After dropping off the passenger, the driver stepped on the accelerator. The handle slipped out of my weak hands; I fell on the street, and my sister screamed while hitting the window with her fist to warn the driver to stop. Courageously, I got up and came back on the *tap tap* with scratches on my hands and knees.

2. The Bus of the Faculty of Sciences

In Haiti, I was a player in the soccer team of the Faculty of Sciences. One Saturday morning, the players and the trainers took the bus of the faculty to the Park of Ste Therese, where the inter-faculty championship usually took place at that time. Once inside the bus we, the adult-students, didn't sit down. We jumped from our seats whenever the bus hit a pothole the same way the little ones jumped from their seat anytime the bus hit a bump in the parking lot of the Wheatley Heights Apartment Complex or any other apartment community. We, the grownups, were singing, cursing, horse-playing, and teasing the bus driver. We called him engineer to identify him to ourselves, or more precisely to humiliate him. Although I and the other students were already adults, we acted the same way, or perhaps worse than the students here, given that the coaches did not really care.

CHAPTER V

The Longue Journey: True Reality Of A Run Or The Story Of Each Stop

Every morning, people see the bus coming to pick up the students to drive them to school. But have you ever thought about the process of a school route and the true reality of each stop? In this chapter, our mission is to clarify and explain to you the story of each stop.

i. From Home to Yard

One morning, I woke up, dressed up, and did my regular routine in order to be ready for work. After leaving home, I drove carefully because it was a cold morning; the pavement was icy due to the overnight drop of temperature. On Pulaski Road, I passed the same jogger. A few feet ahead, I picked up my friend, the Mexican guy. Caring for me, and aware of the noise in my car, he handed me his friend's business card, a Mexican mechanic. He told me, "Roman, he isn't expensive. His shop is located in Brentwood. He'll fix this problem for you."

I took the card and said thank you.

I dropped him off a few feet away from the yard; I arrived at the yard. I did the pre-trip, then I checked with base to make sure they were in connection with me. With the right hand, I did the sign of the cross three times; and I kissed my hand three times, asking God to accompany me on the road.

On my way out, a dispatcher, Frenio, called me. I say, "Que pasa chico?"

Everyone likes him; he is a helpful, smart, hardworking, and ambitious young adult. He left the office, walked to my bus and, for the Valentine Day, handed me a certificate, "which greets all school bus drivers, recognizes, and appreciates our dedication and service to the American School Bus Council."

This certificate represents a symbol of appreciation of our sense of love, our smile to the children, the future men and women of America. I put it on my bag, and then I proceeded to my first stop.

ii. The First Stop

It was 6:35 a.m., a Valentine morning, I was running on time for the first pick up. Two Asian students and one white boy boarded the bus. Another girl from that stop was missing that day. I waited a few seconds more and looked around to make sure she wasn't coming. The Asians, a boy and a girl, were chatting. Perhaps a love story blossomed between them; perhaps they were already in love. I felt that a sensual harmony, a sort of natural symbiosis connected them. Should we ignore the fact that some love stories take place on the school bus, an ideal scene? Aren't they humans? And all that is human cannot be quite familiar to them (Socrates). Each one owns a heart that can show feelings, sensibility, and affection. I felt, at that time of Valentine, at that time of love, something was growing between them. Though later, I realized that I was wrong when the boy told me, during the girl's absence, that she was his cousin.

I proceeded to the next stop. While I was driving, I felt something weighty on my stomach: the idea of my family in Haiti. I have heard many Haitians saying, "They have no family in Haiti." Lie.

Me, I have hundreds back there.

That morning, my mind was wondering about the ones I never had a chance to talk to or to see since I came here. I thought I would call my cousin Bobo and ask him to go to visit and tell them how my love for them is big and immense. Bo, you will tell them that New York is not the Promise Land contrary to what most Haitians, and even some people of the world, believe. Assure all of them that I have a plan for everyone. Tell them that I feel my heart tearing apart anytime I think about them. Tell them that every day, every second, every blinking, I think about them. And I will fight fiercely to change their situation. Tell them that I represent their hope, and I won't let them down.

iii. Second Stop

I continued to pick up the students. Each stop contained a meaning, told its own story, bore a message of love and a sort of connection between Roman, the driver, and the students inside it.

In this one, some students waited inside their parents' cars—some days with the mother, other days with the father. The presence of the parents represented a kind of protection during those cold and dark mornings. I also had to wait for a black girl who always waited for the bus inside. I took a few more seconds longer to look in the direction of her home because I did not want to leave her. When they got on the bus, I took great pleasure to greet them, although they only answered me when they felt to. It is the mode in America. I scanned my mirrors, waved to the parents, and continued to the next stop.

iv. Third Stop: A Symbol of Love

In the street, the pick-up stop was near a stop sign. I recognized this stop sign. Last year, I did route 42, where I used to pick up a woman's daughters. She represented one of the nicest persons I have ever met since I have been driving a school bus. For Christmas, she gave me a greeting card and a crucifix with a school sign and an angel, whose arms are open with the sign "Protect my School Bus." I kept the greeting card, but the crucifix had disappeared since it was on top of the interior mirror of the bus. That gift symbolized her faith.

I will never forget that lady, a living symbol of love. We could say a piece of love. On that day of Valentine, I had a special thought for her. She was charming and considerate, always smiling with her two daughters, a boy, and two dogs. Seeing the five living creatures waiting at the bus stop drew in my mind the image of a bouquet of love. Young, fresh, happy, vivid, colorful, full of vigor, they gave me the impression they have beaten melancholy and neutralized hate around them. They belong to the category of people who we always dreamed to be closed to—people whose company is synonym of joy, peace, love. She stood like a tree of happiness, and each child, each dog symbolized a branch that smiled to us and invited us to join their elixir of life.

The French poet Chamfort said, "Time we spend smiling is best used." It is true in the sense that we can surprise people and entertain them with our good humor, our smile. Nevertheless, I didn't know what reason forced a black boy who lives across from the stop to ask that white lady, "Why are you always smiling?"

She looked at him, opened her mouth in sign of contentment, and responded, "Because I'm always happy."

That mother's image, her smile, and her charm will be always attached to my memory and occupy forever a special place in my heart.

v. Fourth Stop

At the next stop, I picked up three students. On the other side of the street, one boy's father wearing an orange sweater, perhaps a town employee, very often raised the right index finger. I understood he asked me to stop. I responded in my mind, "No problem." I will never let one child behind now. I can even wait longer, given the Half Hollow Hills School District gives us a margin of fifteen minutes after the time. As a school bus driver, my motto is "Fòk nan pwen," meaning "Until there is no more." No student would be left behind.

Oh! Let's go back to the father; he waved to me with one finger. What I love in this gesture is the interest he puts in this act in order to show me how caring he is for his son. He understands that the success of his son represents the success of his family. I looked at this father proudly. If I could leave the bus and shake his hand to compliment him and tell him how I appreciate the valor he places in his son's education, his son's future, I would do it. I wish in his old days, his son will be there to appreciate what he has done, to return to him all the affections and all the good things he has done to him.

But at the same time, one idea struck me: It's the fact that in my childhood, I never had the chance to live a full month with my father. Due to political and other reasons beyond his will, he decided to stay away from Haiti for a certain time until it was safe to go back. If I have good memory, the last time we lived together in the same house was only a portion of July 2000, during my first vacation in Miami. It is evident to understand that, except for the genetic characteristics, I never inherited any manner, any default, in brief any influence from this relation of consanguinity.

Ironically, my children are away from me. They are living in Haiti with my sister-in-law. They have to face the same problems I have endured years ago during my youth. But I hope everything is for the better (Socrates), and soon, they will be with me under my protection. I'm positive.

vi. Fifth Stop

Proudly, I continued the run; I picked up four students in a court. The first one, I only saw his face in December, the day he gave me one envelope, my Christmas gift. During my first days as an immigrant school bus driver, I went through some social and cultural transformations, wherein I had to shape and adapt myself according to the demands of the environment.

My friend, Remus who is a bus driver, is really hostile to the American children's comportment. He wrongly pretended that a gate separated us from them. I told him that they are before all children, so it is our duty to transform our mentality and create an ambiance where they can feel at ease. As tall as they might appear, they are still children. I forgot the author who said, "By changing ourselves, we can make a little difference." In fact, my friend also needs to mold himself to create some ideal conditions of work if he wants to survive and perform efficiently. What's the problem if a student looked away anytime he boarded the bus?

The second student always held many bags in both hands. That morning, he was late. I already left that stop. From the driver's mirror, I saw him waving to me to stop. I waited. While he was rushing to get on the bus, his lunch fell on the grass. Some students laughed. He picked it up, ran, and then boarded the bus.

One student, a big mouth, a loud troublemaker joked, "We love you, Claudy." The students laughed.

The third student was a girl who always waited outside for the bus even during the worst weather conditions. She was a tough girl, ready to brave the cold, the winds, and the rainy days. She symbolized the bold and strong woman who trains herself to fight the existence and face life and all its challenges.

The last girl lived across from the third student. She was lucky because I had to turn around in a cul-de-sac. Most of the time, for not waiting outside and fearing of missing the bus, she had to run through the grass to cut me off. I stopped for her and greeted her good morning. She never answered me. She didn't even look at me. But I didn't care. I am a programmable robot. Anytime students board the bus, my job is to "always smile with a warm good morning."

They rarely looked at me. C'mon, stop complaining about the students' behavior. After all, it is your job, Roman!

That student was a tall, pretty, vibrant, well-manicured girl, who dressed impeccably like an actress. With a refined style and the fever of being young, she always dressed lightly and never wore a coat even on cold days. Curiously, even if that student never responded to my good mornings, on her way out of the bus, she always ensured to say to me, "Thank you. Have a nice day!" Like the Americans say, she did not want to leave like a French person.

When it was time to leave, I scanned the mirrors, and I proceeded to the next stop.

vii. Sixth Stop: The Strange Student

I continued my run. I went up the hill on Dix Highway.

Now at the stop, I had to pick up five students; I turned right on Dudley Lane. The students rushed to enter the bus. They came in front of the curbside, making it impossible for me to respect the "eighteen inch rule." By precaution, I stopped the bus in fish tail. A student coming from behind always passed in front of the line to be first. The heavy built student in front never wrestled with him. Passively, he just let him the first to enter.

Once inside, one of the students from this stop caught my attention. Every morning, that high school student always struggled to find a seat inside the bus. To tell the truth, I sadly watched him through the dome mirror. Sometimes, even after I passed three stops, he couldn't still find a seat inside the empty bus. He forgot that this system of life does not give you a chance; you take it. What kept him from sitting in any place? Was it fear of others, fear of deception, or a sort of embarrassment? Was it a kind of complex? Can we esteem that his reaction was incidence of past bully, whose sequels were still traumatizing him? So many questions that only the specialists of children with abnormal behavior can answer.

At the end, someone might move and give him a chance to sit next to him.

Chance, a meaningless word; we don't sit down by chance on the school bus. We sit down because we have the right to sit. This problem has been solved since the night of time. This is not the purpose of this book. It is like life, like a classroom. We affirm ourselves. Ti Manno, one of the most famous Haitian singers said, "If we have complex, we miss something."

This student had complex, or he neither had the courage nor the will to prove himself. In life, we should take what we need as long as we do not break the law. No one is going to decide to give us. We should do the first step in the path of receiving. Our trouble is if we are living a life of beggar, anytime we receive, we feel diminish. My son it is irresponsible to put yourself in a situation to receive in a world that hates to give. This is a reverse world. At least, the world doesn't give to people in need. We should take what we need. "My son, you affirm yourself. Get on the bus and sit down. Period."

viii. Seventh Stop: September Tip

With this particular stop came a surprise for me. From Dix Highway, I turned right on Dudley Lane. It is really rare to see parents accompany high school students to the bus. Surprisingly, the first school day of

September, a mother accompanied her son to the bus stop. She waited by the door and then said politely to me, "Bus driver, can you go to the court over there to pick up my son?"

"I've to turn around. I've to go there anyway," I responded. While looking at her, I added, "It is not recommended to do U-turn with a big bus in the middle of a street or an intersection."

"Thank you," she said while climbing the steps to give me a twenty-dollar bill.

I bent myself a little on the right and stretched my right arm to reach her hand; I took the money with a smile and said thank you.

At first, people can deduct that she was trying to buy me for twenty dollars. Let me be clear: I'm not for sale. But let us go further; let us reason with a little good sense. In fact, that kind of generosity proved the extent of a mother's love and the importance she attached to her son's safety. She wanted everything to be under her field of vision, the oye masteri (master's eyes); in other words, she needed to be able to watch him from her window while he was waiting for the bus, a way to observe him from the distance, a way to keep him away from the crowd, from the bad influences and from the laws of the streets. Didn't she have her own reasons to be her son's guardian angel?

In fact, from that morning to the last day of school, faithful at my commitment, I never missed the court. Probably, the previous driver just turned around at the intersection. On the contrary that year, that particular stop was registered in the paper work of the school district.

ix. Eight Stop

I continued the run; I picked up a pretty girl with a noble and sinuous walk and a naïve and immaculate face. She always responded to me and always said bye to me when leaving the bus. She always looked at me with a kind of sympathy and a certain magic that connected us. Even if we never shared any other word, I felt that she had some kind of compassion, respect, sensibility, and a desire to make me feel good. As a matter of fact, she knew and understood how important her smile and salutation were for me. She was one among the others who could transcend the American teenage way and understood her bus driver as a product of a different culture or a different style of life, and a result of a different philosophy. Every day, she approached me by her manner to look at me and to understand me even if a world of differences separated us. She just wanted to show me how important I was and how she cared for me as her mother cared for her.

The girl is the spitting image of her mother. Before I closed the door, she watched her daughter with tenderness walking through the aisle until she sat in the back next to another friend, then she waved to her. For sure, she inherited the good manner from her mother.

Now I drove away to the school, and I made a right on Carll's Straight Path. Before I reached Vanderbilt Parkway, I followed the semi-circle where it is usually foggy in the morning. In order to drive them safely to school, I turned, controlled, or crossed over each intersection with all the necessary care. I turned left on Vanderbilt Parkway, my eyes in thousand directions, controlling my mirrors on average every eight seconds according to the rules. The seven mirrors of the bus, the imaginary pentagon as I call them, occupy an important role in the defensive driving system: They help me watch for oncoming traffic, cars behind me, the hazards, and distractions of the roads such as bicyclists, squirrels, joggers, etc.

I glanced at the interior mirror, the dome mirror as it is called, and it reflected the images of forty-four students behind me. At the same time, different things were happening inside the bus. Shhht! I heard the snoring of one sleeper in the first row. That blonde girl behind me had a chat with her friend; some others were texting, some listening to the bus radio. They trusted me as their driver; at least, they were forced to trust me.

Naturally, I trust myself, and I hope that all school bus drivers need to trust themselves. Students do not have any control over their transportation; they have to accept whoever comes to pick them up; it is a parameter independent of their will. No student could pierce the mystery behind any bus driver's mind, since they have no way to verify if he is a sex offender, or if he is drunk, or if he is high in drugs.

I continued down the hill on Vanderbilt Parkway, a right on Deer Park Road and a quick left on Wolf Hill Road. Let me mention that drivers, who are coming out of Vanderbilt Parkwayand want to proceed on Wolf Hill Road, face a challenge if they want to apply the traffic rules. In fact, once we turn right on Deer Park Road, the next intersection is located at a short distance that we just have to cross diagonally two lanes. In such a case, being aware of this particularity, and as the route driver, I violated twice the rules of changing lane. Opting to apply them in that particular case would put me in an uncomfortable situation, where the aggressive car driver behind me would not give me the least chance to go to the left.

I drove down the hill on Wolf Hill Road; the speed of the bus had a tendency to increase due to the force of gravity. That morning, the road was strangely deserted. On my bus, the high school students were allowed to listen to the radio. Meanwhile, I used a simple system to make them benefit from the twenty minutes they would pass with me on the bus. In fact, in the morning, we listened to the news, sports, and other events; in the afternoon, we relaxed our mind with some music. On demand, I switched the frequency to their favorite station. My students liked me; they liked the bus. I cared for them, and I knew, I felt that they cared for me too.

A right to enter the High School West, their school, my school, their house, my house, I stopped; and from the microphone located next to the radio, I wished them a nice day.

Happy to go for the day, all of them got ready to leave. Surprisingly, these students never pushed each other. They were still young, but they behaved courteously. In fact, the school bus is a scene where we meet wonderful students from different classes: rich, middle, poor. Some were orphans, or others might have been adopted. But one thing was sure: Their comportment reflected a direct comportment of the environment where they evolved.

Let me make it clear. School bus drivers face less problems driving students whose parents can participate in school meetings, are available for them, and prioritize their emotional, moral, and social presence to the benefit of their children's lives. As a matter of fact, for that very simple reason and whenever possible (better seniority and not being a spare driver), during the pick, we, school bus drivers, opt for the route that we think could cause the least problem. The hope of better tips, the distance to cover, etc., represent secondary parameters in the pick of a route.

They were leaving the bus one by one. Walking down the steps carefully, the pretty petite girl never forgot to tell me, "Bye! Have a nice day!" even if for that fraction of time, my head was down wondering about thousand ideas. Being a Haitian, I know that anybody who disregards a greeting is impolite and guided by the moral principles attached to this job, I responded to her with all the kindness, all the courtesy, and all the happiness in my heart. Her "Au revoir!(Bye!)" represents a way to let me understand that someone on the bus cares for me and deeply appreciates the job and the service I have done: Drive them safely to school. Her thanks replaces all the other thanks. It symbolizes a sort of universal thanks for all the others who never thank me, or at least for the ones who does not know, or others who did not learn to thank, and for the rest who deliberately does not want to thank.

When the bus was almost empty, I got up to let the last ones go. I told them, "Have a nice day."

They answered me, and then left.

I walked to the back to do the post-trip inspection. I looked for all kinds of things: backpacks, coats, money, folders, cell phones, cigarettes, contraceptive pills, drugs, condoms, books, porn magazines, etc.

You smile, don't you? It's true. All those items, and even worst others, have been found on a school bus after a post-trip.

Post-trip is important and indispensable because we know after the high school, we have to drive middle school students. So young, with no experience, they need more attention. They are more fragile to be a victim; they have more risks to be corrupted and are easier to be controlled or deviated. And for so many reasons, it is an obligation to conduct a post-trip inspection on our bus after each school trip.

I left the high school to continue with the next run. I proceeded to start the middle school. Each stop contained a particular story, a particular complexity, and a particular kind of behavior. I went to pick up the middle school students and then to face other stories; I went to pick up other sentimentalities, other acts of love, other kinds of students, other challenges, and other problems.

CHAPTER VI

Problems With Parents

A few parents do not care about their relationship with their children's bus drivers. Generally, it is evident that they are, in spite a few of them, good collaborators. They represent an important link in the chain of discipline of the school system. My purpose is not to blame some parents for their rudeness, but I do feel the necessity to relate these sinister events that have happened to me while on duty. I have also experienced problems that forced me to raise some minor arguments with five parents, including a pretty serious one.

i. The Lady of Carman Road

One morning on Carman Road, I missed a stop; and the dispatcher called me saying, "Hey, Roman, did you stop at number 7777 on Carman Road?"

I responded, "Oh, I forgot it. I'm sorry."

"Can you go back at this stop?"

"Sure."

I went down on Carman Road, crossed over Wolf Hill Road, and entered the park across. I turned around and went back to pick up the children. When I got there, I apologized to the mother for missing the stop. She gave me a dirty look.

Another day, since the students were inside the house, I missed the same stop. The dispatcher called me and ordered me to go back. I went back that day; the mother accompanied her children to the bus. She frowned and said, "Are you crazy? Are you drunk? Do you do drugs?"

I didn't say a word. I just picked up her children, the quietest ones on the bus, and I proceeded to school.

ii. The Pictures

The second day of that school session, a parent, a mother was, furious because she thought that I had dropped her daughter, a kindergartener, in the middle of the street. As usual, I began the morning run at 8:30 a.m. This Tuesday morning, I had to pick up a kindergartener, a little and gentle girl, in front of her house. Contrary to a corner stop where we have to pick up the students around ten feet before the intersection, that one was a house stop, which means I had to stop in front of the house number. So I stopped, secured the bus, and opened the door. The mother came by the door and said, "Why did you leave my baby in the middle of the street?"

I said, "Pardon me? I didn't drop your daughter in the street."

"This is an area overrun with child offenders. You know what, give me your name. I'm going to call the company and ask them to fire you."

"My name is Roman Blaise. Fire me!"

She stayed by the entrance and blocked the door with her back. To another teenage girl who was standing at the curb, she said, "Bring me the camera."

The girl brought a cell phone, stood in front of the bus, and took my pictures. I wanted to pose for her so I could have my photo taken in different positions, but I was sitting. So I waited for her until she cleared the way. Then I closed the door and moved on.

Obviously, since it was the beginning of the school year, I could understand a mother's fear, suspicions, and prejudice about the bus driver. Now, does taking a driver's picture in this situation the right thing to do? We, as school bus drivers, have to follow a code of ethics. We have to perform our duty with professionalism; we need to comply with a code of conduct and correctly fulfill our mission, which is "to drive the students safely to and from school." Some rules have been established to discipline school bus drivers when necessary. You do not have to give yourself justice. If everyone was allowed to do so, the world would be a place of more chaos and violence. Taking a bus driver's picture in this condition was an indirect threat.

After a few months, I realized that this mother was not living in the address where I picked up the child. After moving to another town, many parents who do not want to switch school district use a friend or a parent's address. That reason explains why she was not outside waiting for her daughter.

Now was my reaction a good one? Absolutely not! I did not react the right way. The right reaction should be, anytime a bus driver feels threatened, he has to hold the microphone and let dispatchers and other drivers know what is going on, or to repeat or alert in the radio the code that translates an imminent danger.

Surprisingly, after explaining to the safety manager about the incident, she told me that she was around. If I had called for help, she would have been there in a matter of minutes.

iii. Late Report Effects

Another interesting case was a mother's reaction after I have reported her kindergartener son. Since school began, I had tried in vain all kinds of tricks in order to convince him to sit down. Perhaps, this child has not been educated about listening and obeying at home. Consequently, I confronted some difficulties to shape him my own way in a matter of few weeks. For the record, and also to draw the parents' attention of the disturbances he has caused on the bus, I reported him.

That report irritated the mother, who became mad at me after she was informed of her son's behavior by the school district. As a matter of fact, she protested, saying that I should have told her immediately about her son's behavior so she could warn him and remind him on how to behave. She pretended that too much time between the act and the warning would have had less impact on the child, since he would not remember why he was warned for.

Was I responsible? It was not my responsibility to carry on with the report until the parent received it. I have done what I was supposed to do.

iv. The Five Hundred Dollars Trumpet

Another serious incident happened on my bus during my first year as a school bus driver. One afternoon of fall 2004, after dropping off the middle school students, I went to Signal Hill Elementary School to pick up other students. I parked the bus next to another one; I took the newspaper from the dashboard and began to read. A male student entered the bus; he said, "Bus driver, I forgot my trumpet."

Obviously, after the post-trip, I found the trumpet in the back and put it behind my seat. I told him, "Do you have an ID so I can verify the name?"

Gently, he responded, "I don't have an ID."

Then I said, "I'm sorry, I can't give it to you."

The boy left.

A few seconds later, a man came by the door and shouted, "Give me the trumpet!"

"OK. Show me your ID, sir," I responded.

Now, he entered the bus, his feet on the stairs. With the right hand, he tried to get the trumpet behind my seat. Then he added, "Give me the trumpet. It's a f-n five-hundred-dollar trumpet."

I was already standing in front of him and blocked the space behind my seat in order to prevent him from taking the instrument. Calmly, I said, "Sir, show me your ID. If he is your son, then you can go with the instrument."

But to be clear, some people stereotype bus driver. My great-grandmother has built my personality. I'm not going to step down when I know I'm right.

Then the father shouted, "If you don't give me the trumpet, I'm going to arrest you because I'm a chief."

I smiled; and I responded, "What are you talking about? Just show me your ID, then I'll give it to you."

Come on! Should I let a chief threaten me when I know the rules? In that case, I had the obligation to do my job like any responsible school bus drivers would. In the meantime, I looked over his shoulder and saw a female teacher, who witnessed the violent argument, running back inside the school. In my mind I thought I could handle this situation. I did not argue with him, but I tried to convince him to finally show me his ID.

As a chief, you should better know the rules than I. Finally, when he was convinced that I was not going to step down, from his pocket he pulled his wallet, took his identification card, and showed it to me. I looked carefully to make sure the last names matched. Now, I pulled the trumpet from behind my seat and handed it to him. He took it then left.

While he was leaving, I saw the principal, a very well-built woman, running to the bus. She asked, "Are you OK?"

I responded, "Everything is fine."

Over the years, experience shows drivers a better way to control these unexpected incidents. Whoever is reading this page now should bear in mind that a school bus driver has to solve new problems very often. It is clear that sometimes problems spice up the dramatic life we are living.

v. The Landscape Drive Drama

To corroborate this, on October 21, 2009, another incident occurred. I covered a 4:15 p.m. Vanderbilt Elementary route. Before I talk about the incident, I have to explain to the reader the circumstances that have led to it.

Firstly, I did not use my method, which was to scan the lefts and rights to check all the addresses of the students on the bus. Secondly, throughout the run, I have made two mistakes that delayed the drop-off time. One, I had to make a sharp turn, but I missed the street, and then I turned around some blocks to come back to my destination. The other mistake was a left turn that took me to a wrong street, given that the name on the sign differed from the name on the paper. Eventually, I went around and got back through side streets.

While doing this route, the third mistake I made was instead of following my judgment and using my own way to do the run, and given the number of elementary students, I decided to follow the Left and Right sheets that the driver handed to me. Not that they were bad. No! I do not have to blame her as I never did. That was my mistake. Therefore, I had to face the consequences.

That afternoon, the consequences would have been grave if I did not control my temper. The consequences would have been a dramatic disaster not only for me, but also for a woman, a student's mother. So many times, as a school bus driver, I have been on the brink of a disaster while doing this job. What has that lady done?

As a matter of fact, that lady cut the bus off while I was driving down Landscape Drive. Through my left sideview mirror, I saw her car coming behind the bus. She was tailgating the bus on the left side. She wanted to pull over in front of me. To prevent any accident, I slowed down. I did not speed. I did not have to block her. I was not supposed to. Remember the hen philosophy (Ref p.68)? I let her pass. She cut me off and stopped in fishtail right in front of the bus. Then she got off her car.

She got off her car; it was normal. Evidently, she rushed and stood by the door to ask me indignantly to let her daughter off the bus. She questioned me for being late. She might have an appointment, or something important to do. Who knows? Was that a reason to make a spectacle of herself in front of the children and the people in the neighborhood? She yelled, "I want my daughter."

"I'm not allowed to drop off your daughter in the middle of the street," I replied.

The daughter said, "That's my mother. I want to go."

"OK. I'm going to drive you home."

"I want to go now."

The mother continued the shouting in the street, and I could hear her voice from the other side of the bus. She stood by the door; with a circular sign with my right hand, I directed her to the driver's window. She did not want to come. I refused to open the door; she might jump inside the bus and, that way, disturbed the atmosphere inside. In this kind of situation, we open the door when we have to. Also, other students might leave the bus. I will be the first one to be *hanged*.

At that time, a concert without harmony took place on the bus. The students began to cry. Some of them wanted to go home; others, already tired, hungry, and exhausted, who did not want to witness this drama, were very upset.

It is important to underscore that the safety rules of the company requires us to make sure we wait for each elementary child to enter the house, or have somebody pick this student up at the stop.

I explained to the daughter that the school district does not want bus driver to drop off students in the middle of the street. The previous year, one driver lost his route after complying to some parents' requests and dropping off some students in the middle of the street. I ordered them to sit down so I could continue.

I continued the run and dropped off some students on Main Avenue. At the intersection of William Street and Jordan Street, the lady who cut me off a few minutes ago came to get her daughter. She shouted, "Let the district's driver bring these poor children home."

She took her daughter, and she asked another white female student to come with her. She said that the girl lives at the next house. I let her go because I saw her mother coming on the other side of the street.

A tall, light-skinned man came by the driver's window. He said to me with a quiet tone, "You realize how stupid you are?"

Calmly, I replied, "How do you know that?"

Another man, a district driver, came by the bus. He changed a few words with the mother who just cut me off. She then turned to say to me, "The school district driver said you don't want to let the children go to his bus."

How did I know that this driver was waiting for me? Did he wave to me? Did he communicate by dimming the lights or by blowing the horn? He is face to his conscience. If he has the chance to read this book, he can answer now. How can I distinguish this school van among all the other vans and buses that were in the area that afternoon?

That school district van driver came by the door and looked at me. I tried to explain the situation to him, but he totally ignored me and went back to his van as if my word did not have any sense, as if my stony French-Creole accent could not impress him. It is normal, when in danger or when we make a mistake in life, sometimes people, society, or even our close friends betray us. When we suffer from an incurable disease and we become desperate, the world abandons us. What about the solidarity that all school bus drivers have to show? How long would it take to just listen to my statement? No patience. I did not ask you to listen to me. At least say something. He did not say anything. I thought he came by the door just to know who that *stupid* school bus driver named Roman is.

But let us analyze deeply the content of some parents' first impressions of Roman, the school bus driver.

a) Are You Crazy? Are You Drunk? Do You Do Drugs?

Three interrogation sentences, a lot of meanings. Three pejorative and revealing phrases to someone who, for a certain time during the day, sustained your child's life. Don't you think that these words can damage our existence? Don't you think that a bus driver might decide, "That's it? You are not going to insult any other bus driver anymore?" Come on! Have a little good judgment. Isn't it an eventuality in this crazy world? For those who believe, let us pray to God that something like that doesn't happen. For the others, let us fight against the bad forces that take over us.

Why do a few parents use all kinds of words to belittle a school bus driver? Do they really think that any company would deliberately hire bus drivers that are crazy, drunk, or drug addicts? Do you think my company would hire someone out of his senses and give him the responsibility to drive your children? Do the NYS Education Department's requirements would clear someone in this category to drive students (8NYCRR 87.4 and 8NYCRR 87.2 h1)?

In the same logical line, a father, the chief, feared to lose his son's trumpet. Listen to what he said:

b) It's a Fn Five Hundred Dollars Trumpet

It is not my problem. It is yours. I am not asking you to trust me. You trust me with your son's life, but you cannot trust me with a trumpet. Let's be serious. Which one is more important?

Hi, brother! My life, my family's life is more important than five hundred misery bucks that can fly or disappear in a fraction of seconds in this expensive life, in this rich and great nation. Do not say something that you will regret all your life. It is right to protect your son's trumpet, and it is legitimate to preserve what you already have—instinct of conservation.

We should also learn to save mutual respect. It is important to preserve someone's dignity. You just do not say what comes from your mouth; you have to balance and measure it before you throw it. If it weighs too much, it can destroy your existence. It might also be a boomerang that can return to hit you and ipso facto hurt you.

Was it an indirect threat or an intimidation under the pretention of being a chief? Or was it an indirect way to say that I am a thief? I don't know. Whatever you wanted to say, (it is natural to be prejudicial) make sure it is based on real foundations. You should learn to see with interior eyes. Do not focus the camera on me because of my silhouette, because of the way I dress, because of my accent, and because of many other unthinkable reasons.

I do not know how old you are. Let me pretend I am older than you, so I had to protect you because you reacted like a child. That day, you did not measure the consequences. In fact, I am sure that when you became mature during the night, you have realized how immense your mistake was. Now, forget about that!

Is it normal for every school bus driver sometimes to face parents' insults when they negligently use all kinds of words? The last one that hurts is the word *stupid*.

c) You Realize How Stupid You Are

Not ignoring the fact that some school bus drivers might be stupid, it is your choice but not mine. But your statement requires certain reserves.

Stupid, a strong word to describe a poor driver. I have to make it clear; some people judge people by their job; some others by their face, some by their size, etc., so many characteristics that can lead them to the wrong path. *Stupid*, a word with different meanings. Friend, we might be living in the same poultry yard, but we don't have the same feather. You do not just assume that somebody is stupid just by looking at him. The shortest and the least attractive man can be endowed with some extraordinary qualities and realizes some unthinkable exploits that touch the humankind's heart. Billions of people have lived on this Earth, but only a few will be remembered. Therefore, we would better pass in this life as a snail. In fact, if we do not want to pass as an anonymous, we should stamp our life with our trace. My friend, twenty years from now you will be more disappointed by the things you didn't do than by the things you did do (Mark Twain). In other words, it will not matter how your hair look, what kind of car you drive...What will matter is what you have learned and how you use it.

Was your intention a kind of prejudice or stereotype? How did you know I'm stupid? I wish I could put you behind the steering wheel of a big school bus, for the first time, to drive some noisy students who do not know you and cannot show you their destination. I wish you could drive a bus full of students with behavioral and emotional problems. Depending on the circumstances, they would choose to naturally make noise either for being nervous, or because they would feel too tired after a full day at school, or too scared. I wish you could feel the pressure behind the steering wheel in those situations. The same as the Jewish teacher who, witnessing his own students behaving badly on the bus, said to me while I was doing a charter to Roselyn Heights a Saturday morning, "Wow! Every day is like that?"

"Yes," I replied.

No matter how articulate you might be, when you have to pronounce some words, your tongue should become heavy. Should you learn to measure them and think of the consequences? Now you might forget what you have said to me. But my friend "Some words hurt and the scars never erase" (Max Lucado).

Stupid. Right! I am stupid. Am I really stupid? It's your choice, not mine. Your statement might be true in a certain way. True, for driving your child safe home. True, because it was the first time I was doing the route. Should I let your daughter go with a woman who told me that she was your daughter's mother, a woman I saw the first time? In this case, anyone can easily cut a school bus off, stop in front of it, stand by the door, and ask for a child. I open the door, she throws a bomb. You get it.

If I survive the bomb—I would be dead anyway—you and the other parents would have baptized me with all the pejorative names that exist. Imagine what kind of sanctions you would have asked against me.

I am stupid because I decided not to run over her when she stopped right in front of the bus. I am the stupid, isn't it bro? I'm stupid because I controlled my temper and tried to prevent a disaster. If you have a little judgment, give the verdict.

Do you think you are the first one who insulted me? No. You are not. I have been under fires so many times. Was I scared? Not really.

By a strange coincidence, while I was modifying this paragraph around 4:30 a.m., a radio station just broadcasted the headlines of the news. One of them caught my attention: A commuter bus driver has been shot by a passenger. Did I think that something similar could happen to a school bus driver? That's possible. It is possible that one day, a parent could harass, shoot, or even kill either me or another school bus driver. Everything is possible in this crazy world.

To other drivers who have a chance to read these lines, continue your way.

Do your job with all that is positive in you. Fill you duty with respect, love, sincerity, prudence, etc.

We are living in a violent country. I repeat it: America is a violent country, a country of opportunity. If we close our wings, if we, as a scary dog crossing another town in search of food, put our tail between our legs, we would not survive. We have to let our wings wide open so that the wind can transport us in a positive direction; we have to lift our tail high like an antenna to capture the wave of success. The world will not give us any chance; we take our chance in this world!

My great-grandmother taught me to respect people and not to be scared of people. Her rude act or his humiliating words did not intimidate me. Most of the time, drivers cut us off. These sensible insults give to the school bus driver's job all its meanings.

These shameful experiences are nothing compared to the happy souvenirs I have had throughout my career as a school bus driver. Do not think that I am living a life of blame on issues that I had experienced with other people. I am not in this category. I just stressed certain things that were not supposed to happen to school bus drivers, since sometimes we were left without any defense. The motive of these complaints is not to hold people responsible of my situation of being a school bus driver in life. Given that, as a human being, "I was born with all the creative urges" (Writing Your Life, Lou Willet Stanek, PhD, p.22); in other words, I was born with eyes to see, arms that can shape my future, and mind to judge and think. Therefore since birth, I was provided with all the potentials every normal creature should earn. No question to make people bring my burden.

CHAPTER VII

The Driver's Responsibility When Driving A School Bus

Any police officer who graduates from the academy receives all the necessary tools that the job requires. But one of these tools represents at the same time a useful instrument and an instrument of death. If the police officer uses it according to the rules, it can do good things to the society: save people life, protect and assist the elderly, serve the people in need, diminish children and women's abuses, prevent extortions, and reduce crimes rate and all kinds of injustice that is eroding our world, etc. On the contrary, if he abuses his power, the gun he has can be a utensil of his own death.

A school bus could be considered as an instrument of death also. After passing the road test, the company allowed us to drive a school bus that could be fatal for us depending on the way we use it. A school bus is not a sport or a racing car. We, as school bus drivers, should not abuse our right by driving the bus incorrectly. Behind the steering wheel, we sustain the life of the most important people in the United States of America, the students. We should do our best to consider, respect, and apply all the rules of safety.

Based on the fact that we are called to drive them around, safety is our main responsibility. One of the guidelines I think everyone should abide to is, do not drink and drive, as driving a bus is not a game. Driving a school bus is not an easy job as it may appear, or as many people may think. We should live a rigorous life and cultivate the sense of discipline. So many drivers and even some instructors have been caught and consequently dismissed after a random drug test. On the roads, school bus drivers should be aware, alert, and aggressive. We should be prepared to defend ourselves against the assaults of other drivers.

Defend ourselves does not mean we have to retaliate. We just defend ourselves to prevent countless and senseless accidents. You would say it is a shield to protect us against the predators. Experience has taught us to be calm and to keep our composure. We know how to behave ourselves and control our emotions when someone cuts us up dangerously, passes on our right, runs straight toward the bus to intimidate us, or commits a mistake whose consequences could be fatal. As I said in another chapter, we are the hen, so let the chicks eat first. That is to say, we should let all the other drivers pass us.

The same as the police officer who uses his gun for people's well-being and for the society's protection, we, school bus drivers, should use our bus cautiously and prevent unexpected mistakes from other drivers. In light of such considerations, we would not sign our death warrant if we make a smart and responsible use of the bus against the hazards of the roads.

CHAPTER VIII

Hazards Or Distractions Of The Roads

School bus drivers should expect to face their biggest problems on the roads. We have seen and experienced the worst cases of traffic violations in the streets. We have to be alert, focused, and aware of the hazards and distractions of the roads such as animals, people in the street, garbage cans, other drivers, sometimes police, and even ourselves. According to the New York State Department of Motor Vehicles (NYSDMV), 21.6 percent of school vehicles accidents were due to drivers' inattention or distraction (Table 7 [P] NYSDMV).

i. Observation

As a little boy, I used to go to the Handicapped Hospital St. Vincent in Port-au-Prince to visit the doctor with my cousin, Joseph Carmeau, who has a hunchback. One day, a blind girl who ran down the stairs caught my curiosity. She strangely and cautiously went around all the obstacles, and she did many turns before reaching the door that gave access to her class. Did she have a kind of sonar? For being in the environment a long time, perhaps since she was a child, she had a large knowledge of all the detours.

I tell the real-life story above to emphasize how the school bus drivers also become familiar with the route and the obstacles on the roads: deformations of the road under the heat or under the pressure of the snow blower trucks, potholes, bumps, etc. We should be like the blind student using the same tools: our reflexes and our experiences of the area. These tools will help us drive safely, protect our passengers and pedestrians, and even save some creatures on the roads.

ii. Creatures on the Road

Among the creatures encountered on the roads, the squirrels are the most at risk. Is it because they have a small brain, as someone used to say? When they see the bus coming toward them, they sometimes put us in a dangerous situation because they dither and confuse us when we have to choose a way to pass in order not to run over them. My reaction is to slow down when it comes to that moment. Cats usually run in front of the bus, diminishing our chance to spare them. Dogs are smarter. Generally, they don't run in front of the bus; they control the situation until it is safe to cross. The chipmunks sometimes run or stop in the middle of the road.

iii. Killing of Animals

I never had the misfortune to kill any animal while driving a school bus. Unfortunately, with my cars, I hit one bird and ran over a chipmunk. Coming from Westbury, I was heading East on Northern Parkway; I passed under a bridge. The bird rushed to cross in front the car. Normally, I thought nothing had happened. Three days later, as I was about to fill up the radiator of my truck with coolant because it was leaking, I discovered the bird's dead body that came across my bumper a few days earlier. I pulled it out and threw it away.

Another case that tore me apart was about a chipmunk. Around ten, after my morning run, I was going home. On my way down Clay Pitts Road, by St. Francis Church, I saw a miniature creature in the middle of the street. My reflexes commanded me to move to the left in order not to run it over because it was crossing from left to right. After passing, I checked on my mirror to see if I didn't hurt or kill it, but I couldn't see anything. Later on my way back, I looked and noticed the torn little body of that animal in the street. I felt guilty that day for not having been able to save that rodent's life, which was necessary to the ecosystem.

iv. The Chihuahua's Death

A morning in Centereach, I witnessed a hideous scene of an accident: the death of a dog. In fact, during a trip to the Riverhead Jail, I had to stop because this sinister event held up the traffic. The dog, a Chihuahua, was lying down on the cold pavement. It was struck by a car that was parked at the shoulder of the Road, the car's bumper on the other side of the street. On the sidewalk, the driver's hand was shaking while she was dialing a number on her cell phone. Next to the dog was a squatting woman, the owner. The animal did not move its frail and bloody body. For its last moment, its eyes were still open to observe human kind's meanness. It probably wanted to shake its tail and let her owner know, for the last time, the extent of its love for her.

Sadly, she just lost a spoiled dog who used to show its love in all its fullness to her; a poor dog that with its tail, its tongue, and all its body used to share its affection and appreciation to her. For a last time, it wanted to bark, but it became voiceless. If I could step closer to it, I would hear its moans. With her right hand, the owner softly caressed her doggy's head. Her warm hand could not force the canine to close its eyes as usual because all its nerves were already disabled after the contact with the car. In a highly emotional state, while her hand was shaking, she armed herself with the courage to close its eyes. She was kneeling there in front of her pet, her companion, her only friend, her bodyguard. She was impassively and painfully observing its final moments and waiting for the time to come, so the dog could go out of its misery.

Before the dog went out of its misery and while its eyes were still open, it gave the female driver a last look which transported shockwaves that probably hit her straight in the heart. In fact, on its way to the other side of the river, it wanted to transmit to the driver a universal message: stop being distracted behind the steering wheel! We can understand that the driver felt a deep sorrow and emotion for pitifully taking away the dog's life. Throughout her existence, she never imagined the possibility of hurting such an animal and sending it to the long trip to the unknown. It is a fact now; the image is still stamped in her mind, and she will live with this horrible memory until the time will also come for her to go to the unknown.

A dog does not have reason, but its behavior has the power to signify to us what love is. Probably, oftentimes during its life, it has been abused, harassed, and beaten up; and to defend itself, it just barked. When a dog cries, it is still OK; when it moans, that means it is really hurt.

They say that a dog does not have any language; it cannot speak, but that one had spoken the language of the heart. They say dog does not talk; that one in its last minute had asked the world for more love, more tenderness, more respect, less abuse, less stupidity, less cruelty, no more war. If any normal dog does not attack a child, why we, as human beings considered better that the animal, harass, rape, traffic, enslave, or destroy children's lives? We are biased in the use of the dog's instinct because we only use its bestial instinct. People only imitate the dog's futile style but not its ethical style.

Finally, the volume of traffic has cleared; I went away from the scene of the accident and proceeded to my destination.

v. Garbage Cans

On garbage pickup days, garbage cans abandoned by the municipal workers litter some main and secondary streets of Long Island, this jewel city.

They often obstruct the roads; and then in order to prevent an accident during the fall and the winter season, we, school bus drivers, have to slow down and use caution. Very often, it is difficult to move around these obstacles when the wind directs them right in front of the bus. I have two choices: One option is to stop and let the wind push them at the curb until we can go in order to prevent them from damaging the bus headlights; the other option is to safely swerve to the right or to the left to avoid the obstacles.

vi. Landscapers

The landscapers represent another dangerous hazard of the roads. Too mindful of their occupation, they use a noisy machine to blow and assemble the leaves, and they are wearing headsets to neutralize the noise. That way, they cannot hear the purr of the bus engine; and as a result, they are not aware of the bus behind them.

Moreover, they do not wear any reflecting clothes to catch our attention during the dark days. We have the responsibility to protect them, since they are potential hazards that all drivers must be aware of.

vii. The Child

A child riding a skateboard or a bike, or running after a soccer ball, cannot measure the danger around him. A child rarely uses his reflexes. On the contrary, he is so busy playing that he even forgets himself. Without any experience, he is enjoying the delights of life; he is in search of adventure and in search of the pleasure that all children enjoy. At the same time, this pleasure can distract him from paying attention. In this sense, he forgets about any other danger and would not see the yellow school bus as visible as it may appear.

Generally, when driving, we are aware of that situation; and we then take appropriate actions to act and save a child's life in case an unexpected incident presents itself before us.

During the spring season, we should be alert vis-a-vis these hazards. When driving in areas of high density of people, the best thing to do is to slow down or stop and try to manage the situation.

A child on a bike almost has the same reaction as a child on a skateboard. Behind the steering wheel, we need to keep a watchful eye in order to protect the children, the future adults of America.

Speaking of adults, how do adult-drivers behave on the roads?

viii. The Biggest Obstacle

The other drivers represent the biggest obstacles on the roads. Whoever is driving a vehicle is considered as a danger: the bikers, the car drivers, the truck drivers, the police, and even other school bus drivers.

All school bus drivers have to struggle with the other drivers' aggressiveness, tolerate their bizarre rudeness, and have to keep themselves from reacting either verbally or showing any inappropriate gestures or accelerating the bus as retaliation.

Most of the time, to react against these drivers' behavior, I used the theory of the hen. What is that?

ix. Theory of the Hen

By experience, I use the hen's comportment with her chicks. Have you ever seen a hen walking with her babies? With her feet, she scratches for food for herself and her chicks, but she does not swallow the food. On the contrary, she lets the chicks eat before herself. Let's say, I am sitting at a restaurant; the waitress brings the meal and serves me. Someone else rushes to take my food. Naturally, I let him take my own meal that has been already served to me.

This should be our comportment. School bus drivers should act like the hen. As mother, she lets the chicks eat the larva. In the same way, we should give way to the other drivers who want to pass us. Do not let ourselves trapped in our gregarious instinct, which dictates us to follow blindly a rude driver just to retaliate against her rude behavior. We will have to yield in situations where we have the right of way. Let the car that comes after us, while we are standing at a stop sign, go if our intuition or our judgment tells us to.

In a one-lane road, by courtesy or to clear the traffic, allow the driver in opposite direction to turn left, even if we have been in situation where some others drivers wanted to curse us for the favor. Forgive them! Do not blast our high beams in their mirrors, or blow the horns as a mark of protestation when they cut us off in a rude manner. The space of time we have used to protest—a kind of distraction—can cause an accident, great damages, and even a disaster. Who knows how many accidents have happened due to our reaction to other drivers' harassment?

Our answer should not be slowing down in front of them after they have blown their horns, but continue driving at a reasonable speed limit and let them pass if this fraction of a minute is not going to contrast with our schedule. Do not try to race the bus in order not to let them pass us. Do not tailgate them, or do not follow them to get their license plate numbers after they have passed the red stop lights that flash when we stop to pick up or drop off the students. Wrong logic!

Be calm on the roads, control our instincts and fear, breathe deeply when we are angry with other drivers. Being angry can force us to step too deeply on the accelerator, forcing the bus to jump, increasing the chances of injury inside the bus and the probability of having an accident. It is a wrong reaction, which can cause us to speed the bus without realizing it.

Being angry can force us to become too aggressive (not ignoring the fact that aggressiveness could be sometimes necessary in situations to prevent an accident).

Remember this: "Never make someone feel bad so you feel good"(Max Lucado, He chose the nails, p. 17). Instead of making ourselves feel good alone, let them feel good so we could feel better. Where is our safety if we evolve in a world where we are the only one safe?

So the next time, or anytime we face these situations, be the hen. Let the people eat our meal, since we already know the reasons of their acts.

CHAPTER IX

The Reasons Of Their Acts

Consequently, if we want to reduce the misfortune to have a fatal accident, if we want to diminish any eventuality of a sad incident, we better act like the hen. Many important reasons required us to act like that, among them are slow yellow bus, pace of life in New York, abuse of our right, etc.

Let us consider before the fact that we are driving a slow yellow bus. Generally, all cars behind the bus tend to pass us even if we dare doing fifty-five miles per hour on a highway where the speed limit is forty miles per hour. Why? Why, for heaven's sake, almost all drivers have the tendency to pass us? In their minds, they assume that the bus will have to stop to pick up or to drop off the students and, because of that, it will cause a certain delay to their activities.

The second reason is that drivers are in a rush, as it is in New York, where the pace of life is really fast. Since they live in a busy state, they are trying to be on time in order to keep up with their everyday routines.

The last reason is that some drivers act deliberately because the bus they are driving has an official license plate or because its color is yellow. We should not overuse our stop lights or move slowly in a one-lane road. These forms of bullies upset and create a feeling of frustration for other drivers, etc.

We, as school bus drivers, are not immune to act in any way we want as some of us used to do. Nevertheless, we should apply the rules and, that way, force other drivers to comply with those rules. We should be a model on the roads, not because we know we have been followed, but because we are adults and professionals. We are drivers of students, and we should have a clear conscience and be reasonable with our acts.

Before we become a driver, the company trains us for months, sometimes even more. Depending on our attitude, they can wait until they feel we are ready to take the road test. After taking the test, they give us a route and send us with an experienced driver for one or two weeks so that we familiarize ourselves with the route we are going to do. When they think we are comfortable enough, then they let us go on our own.

For sure, we have had enough training to act differently from other drivers. Make no mistake about it! Do not think that all school bus drivers display the same model behavior when driving. The reason is simple because before becoming school bus drivers, they were already regular drivers, meaning driving with all their bad habits and regular comportment and bringing all that to the school bus drivers' job.

Comportment of Drivers in General

Joke: I hate being behind people driving at the speed limit (unknown author).

In 2002, my friend's wife used to drive me and her brother to a job in North Babylon. One evening, being late, she asked another teenager boy to drop us to work. At that time, I was new in America, ignoring the traffic reality on the roads. Indeed, along the roads I realized that I was like a bull going to the way of death. I was close to death because I was inside a car driven by one of the most undisciplined drivers I have ever witnessed.

That night on Straight Path, he was tailgating a car so close I had the impression that he wanted to push it to pass. The driver did not give way to the pressure. He cut him off and sped. At the next intersection, the lights were red. He just passed, ignoring all the rules of circulation.

When he dropped me off, I told my friend Georges, "I will never ride a car driven by this guy."

This was one among thousand cases that happen every day on the roads. These reckless drivers are responsible for most of the problems encountered by school bus drivers during a run.

CHAPTER X

Problems With Other Drivers

Almost every day, school bus drivers have to spare at least one or two accidents. We should be prepared to defend ourselves against the other drivers' aggressiveness and rudeness in the streets. I cannot remember how many times I have had to prevent an accident. Some are still engraved in my memory and will never be erased. Thus, I am going to share these scary experiences with you.

i. My First Chill

My first chill happened during the fall 2004 at the intersection of Old South Path Road and Half Hollow Road. On my way to West Hollow Middle School, from Old South Path Road, I had to make a right turn onto Half Hollow Road. The lights just turned green. I released the brake pedals, and because I was going downhill, the bus moved forward. I was about to accelerate when, from my left mirror, I noticed a silver van rushing to pass me on the right. I let it go.

Immediately, a sudden chill crossed my body, and I felt my heart beating faster. A quick look showed me the silhouette of a female driver; her passenger, a baby, her most precious gift in a baby seat. My legs began to shake on the accelerator; my breath became short. I shook my head. I took a deep breath in order to regain control of myself. The students behind me did not notice anything. Arriving at the school, I dropped the students off.

Before breakfast, I took a shot of water to slow down the flow of blood in my body.

ii. The Porche

The next year, around three in the afternoon, I almost run over a car. On Half Hollow Road, I was driving home the middle school students. The bus was moving fast, around thirty-two miles per hour. Suddenly, a miniature car, a Porsche Carrera, pulled out of a driveway. A short distance of one or two feet separated the bus bumper from the car. As Half Hollow Road is a one-lane road, I sprung to the left in order not to run over the car. That move put me in the middle of the opposite lane. The vehicles were parallel, both heading eastbound. I blew the horn to warn him of the mistake. As he saw the bus through his window, he quickly shifted the car to another gear and disappeared in front of me.

After only a few months on the job, I notice incidents like that are commonplace. So any school bus driver who thinks about doing career in this domain has to expect to manage these kinds of unexpected events. Every single day, he will have to face the dangers, the misadventures, and other drivers' mistakes. The rule of thumb is to have the control of the environment and not to get angry when people drive dangerously or do unexpected maneuvers that can be fatal or jeopardize the life of the passengers inside the bus.

iii. Cutoffs

Cutoffs represent another kind of problem that we confront so often. In fact, drivers pass the bus, then after, stop right in front of it.

On a nice afternoon, I was heading South on Deer Park Road. As I passed under the overpass of the Long Island Expressway, I noticed a car speeding in my mirror. Since there was a little gap between the bus and the car ahead, the other car passed me, changed lane right away, and stopped right in front of me at a short distance. Indeed, I decreased the speed gradually to prevent any accident.

It is a must for all school bus drivers to become familiar with this strange and deliberate behavior of other drivers.

Frankly, do regular drivers (car drivers or other commercial drivers) represent the only undisciplined people on the roads? The answer is no. Some school bus drivers contributed also to the dilemma. The following example supports this assertion.

iv. The School Van

Having an accident after completing a route is the worst thing any school bus driver would never wish to happen. Since we will have to spend at least three free hours to follow the Alcohol and Drug Testing proceedings, as a requirement of the 49CFR 382.303 (NYS Laws and Regulations, p. 60). In fact, as a way of safety, given that I was heading back to the yard one afternoon, I did exactly the required speed posted on the road: thirty miles per hour.

Surprisingly, a van from another company, heading in the same direction, stepped over the double yellow lines, passed me furiously on Pulaski Road, Huntington Station. I glanced over to look at the driver's face; he kept his head straight and continued his way. To my astonishment, he was an elderly driver. Ironically, he stopped at the red lights between Pulaski Road and Park Avenue. "C'mon! You didn't have to stop. Just run the red lights," I murmured.

v. The Funeral Cortege

It was 11:00 on a Thursday morning; from the ramp of Exit 60 of the Long Island Expressway, I sped the Suburban of the company to merge into the traffic. As soon as I entered the right lane, I heard a loud horn covering the crunch of the tires gripping on the pavement. I look in the rearview mirror, a woman who seemed to be furious waved to me in a way that let me understand that she was upset because I cut her off.

I moved my eyes in the interior mirror; the emergency lights of her Ford Expedition were flashing, and the car in front of me had also its emergency lights on. Only then, I realized that I entered a funeral cortege.

The traffic was dense due to road repairs in the HOV and in the left lane. Suddenly, with an uncontrolled anger, she switched to the left lane, accelerated, then cut me off. Immediately, to prevent an accident, I moved the Suburban to the right and ran to the shoulder in order to let her truck enter the lane and fit into the tiny gap.

CHAPTER XI

Theory And Practice

i. Definition

A theory is a coherent group of propositions used as principle of explanation for a class of phenomena, or a particular conception or view of something to be done or the method of doing it. On the contrary, a practice is the act or process of doing, using, or carrying out something—the execution (Webster's New Universal Dictionary).

Nevertheless, in view of these definitions, school bus drivers find themselves sometimes in delicate situations. A shocking feeling alters our expectation of driving in ideal conditions. Our judgment, combined with the pressure of the moment, will help us decide how to manage time and speed in order to reach our destination. The following are examples displaying the contrast between theory and practice.

1. A dispatcher calls to remind a driver that he is late.

2. Elderly drivers drive at a speed lower than the speed posted. They want to enjoy their ride by driving cautiously.

3. A young driver is talking and texting; he is lost in a kind of adventure.

4. At an intersection, the traffic lights just turn green. The drivers do not move because they are contemplating a Ferrari. Nobody dares blowing the horn to warn the driver that he is moving too slow. Others are curious to look at the car and at the guy.

5. The left and right handwritings are not perfectly written; drivers have to pick up some stops that were not being mentioned.

6. Our mind is wandering. We make a wrong turn and miss the exit; we then have to go around sideways to come back at destination.

7. It is 7:00 a.m., and we are running ten minutes after the departure time. And so on…

In fact, our actions on the roads were supposed to be translated as pre-given results based on sound reasoning and knowledge transmitted to us by a trainer. On the contrary, the aforementioned examples represent, among others, some inconveniences that can cause a run to be delayed. In reality, they sometimes put school bus drivers in opposite situation of what he has been taught during training. Oftentimes, our actions on the roads betray hundred hours of training we have undergone, because a world of differences separates theory from practice. As Yogi Berra puts it, "In theory, there is no difference between theory and practice. In practice, there is."

Moreover, Emmanuel Kant stipulates in General Systems, "Practice without theory is blind. Theory without practice is sterile." Any practice that is not supported by a solid theory is dangerous, and any theory not confirmed by practical experiences is inadequate. They complete each other, walk side by side, and they are two important parts of a whole. You would say two wings of the same bird. If one is missing, the other performs inefficiently.

Although they sometimes contrast, depending on the circumstances leading to their implementation, in them "we find two dimensions, reflection and action; they are in such radical interactions that if one is sacrificed even in part, the other immediately suffers" (Paulo Freire). In an ideal world, their application would create a perfect harmony.

ii. Mystery of the Job

Dear readers, let me share with you an observation I have made during my first months driving a school bus. The first route I did was Smithtown Christian, a school located a few miles north of the Kings Park Yard. After dropping off the students, I proceeded to begin my next run in East Northport, where I had to pick up other students and bring them to Dickenson Elementary School. In fact, being new on the job, I drove carefully, followed the rules, and respected the speed posted. Suddenly a dispatcher called, "Base to 777, Roman."

"Seven seven seven on. Go ahead, base," I replied.

"What's your location, Roman?"

"I'm on 25A."

"How long before you get to the first stop?"

No Answer.

For me, I felt that nothing was wrong, since I had to drive a distance of two to three miles before I reached the first stop. Therefore, I kept driving at the same pace even if I was running fifteen minutes late. Looking at the time and realizing that I was very late on my schedule, my trainer, another driver, ordered me to pull over. She decided to take charge and finish the run. I moved to a passenger seat; she jumped behind the steering wheel and flew on the roads ignoring all the rules of safety, the good instructions, and the life-saving advice she gave me during training until she finished that run.

Her reaction behind the steering wheel let me perceive and understand the mystery surrounding that job.

iii. The Contrast

The power of the logic, our judgment, and the surrounding pressures can force us to do things and even act in a way beyond our control. In fact, my trainer used to explain to me the principle of changing lanes, stop signs, traffic lights, speed control, Smith System, etc. Though in practice, the constraints of time and many other reasons force us sometimes to act in direct opposition of what we have learned during training. Some days, I felt shocked to observe other drivers, even I, apply a totally different approach from the lessons we were taught during the learning process. What a contrast!

Let us analyze some different patterns and signs of the traffic to have a better understanding of the reality.

iv. Stop Sign

We usually follow the rules: Stop 1, 2, 3; look on the left, right and left again; then go. In some situations, depending on the traffic flow, we have to repeat this sequence more than once. Most drivers stop for a stop sign. Sometimes, we would better spend more time at a stop sign, giving the right of way to other drivers if we feel he is in a rush or if we are going to stop at the next block.

During a refresher in August 2006, I heard one safety employee stipulate, "At a stop sign, any driver who sees another car coming should wait until he ensures the car is stopped. That way, he does not leave out any chance for an eventual accident." Doesn't it make sense?

The same way it makes sense to control our speed on the roads.

v. Speed Control

One friend told me, "On my first date, I did ninety miles per hour with my BMW on the 495 Long Island Express Way while my girlfriend was sitting in the passenger seat."

"And what did she say?" I asked him.

"Nothing. I wanted to make sure she trusted me."

Eventually, she became his wife.

This is a way to explain how some drivers enjoy speeding. I smile when thinking about speed limit. It is a fact that if all drivers respected the speed limit on the highways, there would be too much traffic congestion. The police, the technicians in circulation are aware of that. That is why the law enforcement agents rarely give tickets to people who go three to five miles over the speed limit. Some drivers or, even school bus drivers, do not hesitate to go ten to fifteen miles over the speed limit. Others drivers adopt this motto: never behind.

Our motto, as school bus drivers, is to keep the bus at a reasonable and intermittent speed very close to the posted speed limit. Speeding is a dangerous option; in 2008, 6.4 percent of school vehicle accidents were a consequence of unsafe speeding (Table 7[P] NYSDMV, 2008).

Contrary to my friend's behavior on the date, some retired, elderly, or thoughtful drivers drive below the speed limit. They like to enjoy the pleasure of their old days and ensure that one day, they will die peacefully somewhere but not while driving. Some school bus drivers, in order to clock out later, killed the time by driving under the posted speed even when the road conditions are ideal.

We should drive under the speed limit when the road conditions, the traffic, the police, our emotional distractions, or other reasons beyond the spectrum of our will force us to do so. Otherwise, we have to keep an average speed very close to the speed posted if we don't want to be yelled at by some drivers, pushed by others whose blood content have a high concentration of caffeine, or even run over by drivers who are high in other drugs. Isn't that also a possibility?

Ironically, one afternoon on Straight Path Road, I was followed by a safety supervisor and I was caught speeding in a school zone. I wasn't doing ninety miles per hour, but I went over the posted speed limit of the school zone. So I was warned, and I was warned for some good, necessary, and important reasons. That warning represented a seed to grow my character and stop me from doing something out of character. That warning will strengthen my sense of duty so that I fulfill my mission with more respect of the rules.

To my friend, the next time the police catch you doing ninety miles per hour, they would not think you deserve to be trusted. Don't let the excitement of a new adventure cause you to act like a child.

vi. Do not Abuse Your Right

One day my friend, who used to drive a school bus for another company, told me, "Yesterday morning, I caused a lot of traffic on Pulaski Road."

I responded, "Why? Why for God's sake have you done that? It isn't fair."

He added, "The drivers in New York are always harassing us. They are not patient. Yesterday, I played them. I opened the door, displayed the stop sign for almost three minutes for every stop until I decided to move."

"And what were the reactions of the drivers behind you?"

"Some of them were honking their horns. Some took a shortcut, while some others stayed impatiently behind me."

"Are you proud of your act?"

"What you mean?"

"This is New York, my friend! Don't you know the pace of life here? Life is running so fast. Can you count how many people are going to be late at work because of you? A surgeon, a firefighter might be behind you. Some important people might be suffering due to your indifference to other drivers. Can you assume that some drivers will have to double their speed in order to catch the three minutes they lost every time you have made those stops this morning? They will have to rush in order to be on time at work, or at an important appointment, or a job interview. Bro, this is not professionalism. Can you predict how many tickets some drivers behind you are going to get? How many accidents can happen because of your lack of concern, accidents that can be fatal? Are you proud?"

My friend, as school bus drivers, we should put ourselves in the other drivers' shoes to understand that other aspect of the job. I agree that we cannot pull over after each stop to let the drivers behind us go. I understand that we might be late. Sometimes when the demands of the moment required it, a delay of one or two minutes is not going to make us so late.

Pulaski Road is a very busy street during rush hours. When stopping, you can pull over to the shoulder to pick up a student. You must go to the shoulder to respect the "eighteen inch distance" between the bus and the curbside, leaving no space for even a bike or a dog to pass. Indeed, depending on your will, if there are too many cars behind you, let them go and continue on as long as this is not going to contrast with your schedule and make you late.

You know that we, the school bus drivers, as well as managers, regular drivers, police, etc., suffer from "the syndrome of the yellow" (Ref. p.84).

For safety reasons, all school buses are provided with "stop signs with red flashing lights" on the left side. As a matter of fact, those stop signs should be used only for a safer loading and unloading of passengers.

No school bus driver has the right to overuse them and, thus, abuse his right by keeping other legal tenants of the road from freely going about their business.

vii. Traffic Lights

School bus drivers, contrary to other drivers, need to pay more attention to traffic lights. Green lights signal us to continue our way; yellow lights tell us we should be prepared to stop. But what about a red traffic light that just turned green?

We have witnessed some strange behavior while driving a school bus. To prove my point, here is a story that occurred on spring 2007. I was on Carll's Straight Path waiting for the red lights to turn green when I saw a Jeep Cherokee going the opposite direction on the South Service Road. That is why when the lights turn green, we have to look, look, and look.

viii. Red Lights or Blood Lights

Truly, it is commonplace seeing drivers taking red lights on different occasions in the streets of New York. Even if we feel remorse after passing a red light, ironically, the car behind us passes also. And as a direct consequence, 4.3 percent of school vehicles accidents are caused by drivers who disregard traffic control (Table 7 [P] NYSDMV).

Experience, good judgment, and the dangers of the roads teach me to sometimes interpret red lights turning green as a full stop. To illustrate this, let me share with you, dear reader, some scary experiences I made and other traffic violations I witnessed while on the roads.

ix. Road Test

In accordance with the DMV, on my first Biennial Behind-the-Wheel Road Test, Telucia, a well-disciplined and experienced safety manager, took me to the roads for a driving test. After the pretrip inspection, she ordered me to drive back to the yard. While I was driving, she gave me some salutary advice and some true techniques of the roads; she taught me some tricks and some important safety tips. A particular one kept my attention and still helps me when I am driving. If she did not remind me of those tips, perhaps now I would be the past. It was a good one, if not the best, I have learned during my career.

That day, at the intersection of Burr and Townline Road, I was waiting for the green lights in order to turn left on Townline Road. Telucia, the trainer, told me, "Roman, this is a dangerous intersection. When the lights turn green, make sure you count 1, 2, 3. Look before you go because the trucks drivers usually don't stop for red lights when going down the hill. They just honk the horn, then go." Indeed, by pure coincidence, when the lights turned green, I was counting 1, 2…Before I even finished to count, I saw a driver of a big eighteen-wheeler blowing the horn to pass the red lights.

Stunned and still shaking, with her face red, Telucia told me, "Here you go, Roman! You see what I just told you."

That was not the only mysterious behavior I had witnessed on the roads. The following one needs to be also underscored.

x. The Exception

One afternoon of December 2008, on my way back to the yard, a car cut me off on Cedar Road in Commack, by the Jewish Academy School. Normal reaction of the driver! That had happened more than a thousand times. The driver continued until he reached the red traffic lights at the intersection of Cedar and Townline Road. He stopped, looked left and right, moved a little forward, and then surprisingly, at his own risk, run the red. That was an exception. That was not normal.

This driver's comportment did not appear normal because the lights were functioning properly, and he was driving around a school zone, which means he had more chance to get caught by the police.

xi. The Ultimate Red Lights Case

This ultimate and crazy case refers to a strange driver who was zigzagging on Deer Park Avenue. That morning, I was waiting for the green lights at the intersection of Deer Park Road and the North Service Road of the Long Island Expressway. Suddenly, a car heading South on Deer Park Road just appeared. The driver lowered the speed, looked left and right.

Two cars headed toward him, each one in its respective lane. The crazy driver passed the red, engaged in the middle, then stopped. One driver in panic blew the horn, swerved around him in order to prevent a crash; the other car moved to the left to avoid the accident. Now, the road was clear; he raced and passed the red lights, the blood lights.

What were the reasons to jeopardize his life and at the same time put other people's life in danger? Was it a good reason? I do not know. He alone can answer that question.

Now, do we, as school bus drivers, pass red lights or blood lights while driving a school bus? Sometimes yes. In what circumstances?

I entrust with you, my school bus drivers, friends, and colleagues, the task of answering that important and pertinent question.

xii. My Case

On different occasions, I have found myself in situations where I had to pass a red light. Basically, I have taken some blood lights, but the ones I am going to share are memorable.

The first one happened on a hot summer afternoon while I was doing a charter to Port Jefferson. On my way back to the school, five people, including myself, occupied the van. On 347 as marked on the sign, the van was moving exactly at fifty-five miles per hour. The lights just turned yellow; I covered the brake pedals to stop the vehicle. It did not stop right away; it slid on the pavement and stopped in the middle of the intersection of Route 347 and another street. Without the least hesitation, I kept moving and passed the red lights.

The second one occurred in Commack Road; that day, I made a right turn on the North Service Road with the safety truck of the company. The lights just turned red, but I did not wait for the three seconds imposed by the new traffic regulations. Therefore, I was nailed by the cameras they had just installed. I was obligated to pay the fines.

Obviously, humankind is able of doing all kinds of excess. We, as school bus drivers, should not consider ourselves immune because we drive a yellow bus, or because two official license plates hang on the bus bumpers. We should not make it a rule of doing what please us and act in a way that disgusts other occupants of the roads. In short, "as a shepherd, we should not eat the sheep," to repeat the ex-Haitian President Dumarsais Estime during his inaugural speech.

We know this Latin quote, "Errare humanum est (It is human to commit mistakes)." Honestly, we have made some mistakes on the roads. Let say it directly. We have taken some red lights. Some because we were too close, some due to lack of concentration, and others by simple oversight that could even cause our death.

Many reasons can force us to run the red lights. One thing is important: Under no circumstances we should make it a style of life.

CHAPTER XII

Harassment On The Road

A bus driver should be strong in order to absorb the pressures and the harassments of other drivers.

i. Crisis of Anger

In the afternoon, bus drivers have to be really careful and vigilant. The ambiance at the high school is crazy; people are in a rush. For being hungry, some want to get home quickly in order to take dinner; others have to go to the next job, and they need to catch the train or the bus. That man does not want to miss an important date with a divine girl; some others even rush naturally for no apparent reason. After all, it is New York!

On June, 2007, the last week of school, I picked up students in High School West. That afternoon, my bus was full and ready to go. I released the emergency brake and then switched the radio to 106.1 to relax the students with some beautiful music. I moved forward just about twenty feet. On the curbside, one impatient female student was about to cross to go to her mother's car parked on the other side of the parking lot. By simple courtesy, I stopped to clear the way, and I put my four ways on in order to warn the driver behind me. The girl left the curbside and was walking toward her mother's car. In a crisis of anger, the driver behind me overtook and passed my bus. She was angry because I stopped in front of her.

The girl, like most high school students, was crossing without looking even if we always warn them to watch before crossing. Now, the other bus became parallel with my bus. Suddenly, the driver noticed the girl and stopped abruptly to avoid hitting her. The female bus driver let her go, and then continued her way.

I think this atrocious act haunted her spirit for days, even months.

ii. Tailgating

Another example from my company happened a morning around 6:15. In fact, a spare driver was closely tailgating a Spanish driver, Frederico, on Townline Road in front of Commack High School. The spare driver, ignoring he was driving in a school zone, complained on the radio, "I can't drive behind someone who is doing twenty miles per hour."

The Spanish driver answered with a curse in Spanish. A dispatcher heard the obscenity and then warned Frederico, "Behave yourself."

In fact, curses are not allowed on the radio. A bus driver is also not allowed to harass his colleague. There are different other ways to communicate with another driver such as blowing the horns, dimming the lights, etc.

Tailgating is a wrong and hazardous option because 17 percent of accidents were caused by drivers who follow too closely (Table 7 [P] NYSDMV, 2008).

iii. Syndrome of the Yellow

Dear reader, before I develop this portion, let me share a little joke with you.

Joke
Jesus and Peter were playing dice. Peter threw the dice, and they counted twelve points. He knew for sure that Jesus cannot win, since twelve is the highest score people can make in this game. Jesus took the dice, looked at the sky, said two words, and threw them. They marked thirteen points.

Peter, feeling discouraged, protested kindly to Jesus. "I can't believe this. Even in the game of chance, You're doing a miracle."

In this context, drivers do all kinds of miracles to pass the school bus, the yellow bus. It is the only vehicle that almost all drivers, even I, don't like to follow. Why? Because in our mind, we assume that this yellow box (national school bus chrome) moves too slowly. If we stay behind it, we could be late for our daily activities. Because of that, we put the school bus drivers in delicate and dangerous situations that can jeopardize the passengers and the students' lives on the bus.

We should be always on the alert. As the hen, we should undo the Earth and let the chicks eat, but also watch for predators.

Here's an example. One afternoon, I witnessed a case on Bagatelle Road. A car was caught in the same lane between my bus and another school bus.

Soon the lights turned green; the car's driver moved to the left in order to pass the bus ahead. The bus driver from my company sped and did not let him pass. I condemn his reaction for all the factors enumerated before: slow bus, pace of life, fear of the yellow, etc. We should never let ourselves taken inside this trap. We should never put ourselves in a situation where we have to race the bus with another car. What would we say in case of any preventable accident? What would be the consequences in case of injuries due to our irresponsible behavior behind the steering wheel? What kind of protection would we have against the system?

Let us be responsible even if the other drivers act irresponsible. The next behavior explains that.

iv. The Middle Finger

A close observation shows that most of the time, our children learn their first curse in school. A little girl that my mother used to babysit since the girl was three months old cursed the first day she came back from a daycare. That day, my nephew was teasing her; she reacted by giving him the middle finger. Normal reaction!

During summer 2008, a driver's reaction was the same. That morning, I was heading north on Burr Road, Dix Hills. One car behind was tailgating the van. The driver was impatient; he wanted to pass, so he dimmed the high beams and blew the horns. No shoulder in this street. I searched for the least shoulder's space that could fit the van so the car can pass.

Before I found a safe spot, at his own risks, he decided to pass me. Anyway, after passing me, with his middle finger, he drew all unthinkable gestures; and the images were visible and palpable. The way he moved his hands transported me to a state where I had the feeling that a live basic human act was displayed in front of me. I didn't even react. I was not supposed to.

Thank God I already knew how to control my anger in difficult situations when driving a school bus. For that reason, I advise nerve-racking people not to adventure themselves in this tricky and delicate job. Every day, we will have to face the aggressiveness of other ordinary drivers or even some commercial drivers.

Remember, we are all human beings. Human beings have always caused problems since the dawn of humanity. We not only need to be managed with loyalty, love, and respect; but also, we sometimes need a gendarme with a stick in hand to lead and force us to follow the rules. One Haitian politician used to talk about flexibility and firmness. A mix of both gives birth to a good cocktail.

Getting angry easily behind the steering wheel could be fatal for us one day. In my neighborhood in Haiti, the owner of a restaurant died after a crisis of anger because a customer offered her a trivial price for a meal. Should we let a simple event, due to the syndrome of the yellow destroy our day or our life?

At the end, anytime we're behind the steering wheel of a school bus, we should have in mind that all drivers want to pass us even if we irresponsibly choose to do ninety miles per hour on a fifty-five-mile-per-hour highway. They would drive one hundred, or even over, in order to pass us. The syndrome of the yellow would force them to do the impossible. Like Jesus, they would have to win even a desperate game. In order to pass us, they would do all kinds of miracles.

CHAPTER XIII

The Surprises On The Road

A school bus is built with a set of materials: iron, rubber, glass, steel, etc. As a whole of multiple elements, it is not perfect. Sometimes the system can fail and unexpectedly leaves us in the street.

During my career as a school bus driver, my buses have had numerous breakdowns while on the roads. Among them are leaking problems, brake failure, engine failure, battery, low pressure, and no heat.

Let's talk about three surprises that happened to my bus while I was driving.

i. The First Breakdown

On my first month as a school bus driver, I was driving a van eastbound on Jericho Turnpike in Smithtown. On my way down the hill, I passed under the overpass, right before the statue of the bull. The traffic was dense. A car cut me off and stopped a few inches in front of me. I covered the brake pedal to stop the school van. It didn't stop. Quickly, I shifted it on the lowest gear, made a right turn, and pulled into a driveway. The van still kept moving and was about to plunge in the Nissequoque River. As a last resort, I pushed the emergency brake to stop it.

Ouf! It stopped at last.

Smoke and vapor escaped from the hood.

To protect the children from being injured, I ordered them to quickly leave the van, and I directed them to the other side of the parking lot. I took the fire extinguisher, looked under the engine, then opened up the hood. Instead of fire, vapor was rising from the radiator due to a broken hose. Ensuring that an explosion was not about to occur, I went back inside the van to communicate with base and explain them about the situation. Twenty minutes later, a mechanic brought me another van. Then I drove the students to school.

That was my first surprise on the road. The second one happened two years ago.

ii. No Heat

During wintertime, when it is extremely cold, the mechanics used to start the buses to let the engines warm up before we leave the yard. One morning, the heaters on the bus were on; and I could hear their engines blowing the air, though it was cold inside.

In principle, I have to mention that some buses do not get warm unless their engines are idling. That morning, I left the Kings Park Yard and proceeded to the first pick up. After crossing over Jericho Tunrpike, I noticed that the air inside the bus got even colder.

I began to pick up the high school students. Evidently, the more students got in, the warmer the bus became due to the calorific exchange. During this period of time, the air inside became more comfortable for me, as a Caribbean man, to drive.

Once I dropped the high school students off, the bus became cold again. That winter morning, my warm outfit couldn't protect my body from the cold that crossed my bones, and all my body was shaking. I could not even feel my legs. I decided not to complain. I made a commitment to myself: I'm not going to call. Therefore, I did the high school, the middle school, and the elementary school until I finished the route.

I returned to the base, wrote a defect sheet, asking them to fix the problem.

One morning, I witnessed an elementary girl throwing her jacket to the curb after she has been forced by her mother to wear it. It would be better if all the parents ensured that the little children dress warm when getting on the bus during the winter season. Some students dress light because they believe that the bus will be always warm. Nevertheless, a surprise can happen, the bus can break down, and the space of time before a spare bus comes can cause a sudden change of temperature that could have disastrous effects on a child's health.

What can happen when the low pressure warning signal, the wigwag, fall?

iii. Low Pressure

That winter afternoon, the "wigwag" felt. All big bus and heavyweight truck drivers interpret this defect as a low pressure warning. The most urgent thing to do is to pull over and call base. If not, in a few seconds, the bus would stop automatically.

Cautiously, I stopped the bus in a secured place. It was cold, and because I had a crowded bus with elementary school students, I left the engine on for a few minutes in order to keep the bus warm. On the contrary, cool air was coming out of the heaters. Since the bus broke down in the neighborhood where the students lived, soon many parents came around the bus to pick up their children. I explained the situation to a dispatcher who consented with me to let some of the students go with their parents. After a few minutes, a school district bus picked up the rest of the students and drove them home.

Now, I was the only one inside the bus waiting for the mechanic to bring me another bus. That was a real cold experience!

iv. Surprise Inside the Bus

Depending on our emotional character, any little thing inside the school bus or any minor action can surprise us. And the students smartly use these surprises to act according to our comportment toward them. In this context, the list of objects they use to trap or to tease us changes very often: bear, animal, seatbelts buckled together, slap in the head, pellets, and so on.

v. The Green Snake

One school day of January 2008, I was so stunned that I almost swallowed my tongue. While doing the post-trip inspection, I discovered a green snake on a seat. It looked like natural. Surprised, I ran back to the front. My heart was beating and my breath was short. "Come on, Roman! You are a man," I murmured. Then I came back with the broom, my hand shaking. Cautiously, I touched it with the broomstick to make sure that it was a fake one.

Ironically, we, school bus drivers, should be aware and prepared for these little surprises if we don't want to go into cardiac arrest. This kind of aggression was done by the students either on purpose or by oversight.

Some surprises can be more direct as the next one shows.

vi. The Wood Chips

It happens that drivers who have built an intimate connection with their students have more chance to be harassed or, let's say, preferably teased by them.

One Friday morning, my bus smoothly spiraled up and down through the path of Vanderbilt Parkway. Focused and happy after a cup of coffee and with the hope of a big check because the previous week was a busy one, my head straight on the road, I somehow felt that something good was about to happen. Something good happened indeed!

A twist—a pellet, a missile hit me straight on my head. Who was that pitcher? I scanned the mirror in order to discover the attacker. No one appeared suspicious. I did suspect who did it. I had no right to accuse anybody. No proof. At that time, the buses were not yet equipped with cameras. I decided to forget about that incident, and I did not even dare talk about it, fearing of putting myself in a ridiculous situation.

Once we are in a situation where a student hides himself after a wrongdoing, we almost gain control of our bus. When they are in a state where they feel comfortable to tease us without the least fear, then it is because they feel closer to us.

In particular, there was no reason to pay too much importance to such a surprise as long as the pitcher was not intended to hurt me physically as the next case shows.

vii. Seatbelt

In fact, a driver from my company almost broke his knees while he was post-tripping his bus. Students can't realize how dangerous it is when they join the belts from two seats in opposite row, blocking the aisle. Here is what happened to one retired Haitian school bus driver.

During a post-trip inspection, he walked back in the aisle to check for sleeping students. He did not pay attention to the floor, or perhaps it was dark inside the bus. He did one step and got his two feet blocked and wrapped by the straps. Not having any balance, he plunged. On his way down, his head hit the top of a bench, and both knees brushed the corner of a seat, and his whole body fell on the narrow aisle. The bus balanced under the impact. He got up with bruises, scratches, swollen knees, etc. A few weeks later, he moved to a district job.

As a human being, what is my position to this situation? To be frank, my first reaction was to laugh. Sorry!

Let us analyze it first as a bus driver, then as a child.

No school bus driver would probably agree with that. I sympathized with my friend and coworker, and I shared his pain and his suffering. As a bus driver, we should keep a certain distance from the students. We do not consider ourselves their enemies but on the contrary, a distant friend, an old friend to share their feelings, their joy, and their folly as long as they do not cross the limit.

Some school bus drivers have the magic to transcend a child's fear and become a respectable protector, an alter ego, an inspiration, a model for life, etc. Once we reach this dimension, they will not hurt us. They will cry for us on the last school day, fearing to never see us again.

A child does not analyze or measure the consequences of his actions. He might do it just for fun, not to hurt the driver. Maybe the bus driver was too mean as some of us are.

One afternoon, I heard a boy's remark about another driver who was parked next to me at Candlewood Middle School. "This driver is mean, and he never smiles."

They might hurt us if we never smile, never talk to them, or never empathize with them. They might hurt us if we are too tough and act carelessly. Does fastening the seatbelts together a kind of retaliation? Children always feel delighted when teasing adults. All of us have been children; therefore, we should now understand them.

CHAPTER XIV

Fear While Working

i. Nightmare

One night, I had a nightmare in which the bus flipped over with me. I woke up sweating, with shortness of breath and fast heart beating. That night, I woke up and could not sleep again. Was that nightmare a bad prediction that translated the imminence of a sinister event? Until now, I still do not know the causes. I hope it is for the sake of a cause. Actually, I would not venture myself in this complex task of explaining the motives of such nightmare. Let the mission go to other philosophers who have already speculated in that matter and, in particular, to Sigmund Freud or Carl Jung who consider "dream as the influence of the result of thinking on our subconscious or a kind of interaction between the unconscious and the conscious" (Interpretations of Dream).

For not having a way of revealing the complete meaning of such a dream, and because "our ears should not be bigger than our head" (Haitian quote), that morning, I took all the necessary precautions behind the steering wheel.

ii. Fear

I followed the advice of the night to control my fear. Fear, an emotional state intrinsic to everyone, had also haunted my spirit as a school bus driver on every day's life. The list is long:

1. The fear to crash with another car, or the fear to have a fatal accident.

2. The fear of a mechanical failure that could cause a horrible disaster leading to injury or death.

3. The fear the bus slides one snow day and flips over.

4. The fear of leaving a child on the bus one cold day and imagine what the consequences would be.

5. The fear of injuring or killing a child (either by my negligence or parent's negligence) as it has been the case for many other school bus drivers (22.5 percent of children killed or injured by school vehicles were between five and thirteen years old, Table [9] NYSDMV, 2008).

6. The fear of braking hard one day and causing a child, who is standing in the aisle, to be propulsed to the windshield.

7. The fear of a pedestrian putting his foot on purpose under the tire of my bus with the hope of a couple-of-million-dollar lawsuit.

8. The fear of a terrorist.

9. The fear of directing the bus on a parkway while daydreaming.

10. The fear of any distraction or hazard.

11. The fear of an unknown incident.

12. The fear that another normal driver or pedestrian, being weighed down with the burden of life, decides to run under the bus and says, "That's it! I'm going to make this driver execute me."

13. The fear to sleep one day while driving.

These emotional states represent strong possibilities that have already happened, still can happen, and will probably happen one day either to us or to one of ours. The simple thought and the eventuality of such incidents to happen, and the consequences and sanctions relating to them, leave a sour taste in my mouth.

iii. Sleeping Behind the Wheel

To stay awake and alert, some school bus drivers drink many cups of coffee every day; others take vitamins or stimulants. I usually have one or two cups of coffee in the morning, but coffee itself cannot keep us awake the whole day. Our body and mind have to get used to the routine until we become comfortable anytime we are driving.

In the Faculty of Sciences of Haiti, I remember after spending six nights preparing for the exams of end session in the architectural laboratory, the seventh night, I drank a sixteen ounce cup of coffee. Nevertheless I slept like a baby the whole night on a table until a student woke me up the next morning at 7:00 a.m.

Sincerely, during my first year as a driver, after lunch, I have been in situation where I tried hard to be focused and have a full control of myself to direct the bus to its destination. I had to fight against some states of drowsiness before my body got adjusted to the new driving routine and I was able to use it with its full efficiency. Once I got used to it, it was not a problem for me to drive all day with very short breaks in between. As a matter of fact, two incidents—the results of drowsiness—that have happened to me during my experience as a school bus driver, still drew my attention.

The first incident occurred to me in January 2005; I brought the bus home that day. Traditionally, Haitians take dinner at noon. After dinner, I drove the bus to the school.

At 2:12 p.m., I left the High School West; I drove down Wolf Hill Road, made a right turn on Deer Park Road, took a quick left on Vanderbilt Parkway, and then turned right on Carll's Straight Path. Now, I felt my eyes begin to close; I managed myself to follow a dangerous curb on the street. The need to sleep took over; therefore, I drove slowly. My eyes were closed intermittently, then they opened and I saw a street coming up. Right away, I turned left. Oh! Oh! Wrong street. For not being attentive, I thought this was the street I had to begin to drop off. No, it wasn't. The houses, the architecture, the panorama looked different. I went inside the cul-de-sac to turn around.

In a sign of guilt, I looked at the students in the mirror. They didn't say a word. How could I get lost while doing my regular run? Perhaps, they understood what was going on; I have been a student also. Since then, this little mistake has kept me awake.

I ran around the block and successively dropped off the students at their stops. This incident has since been engraved in my memory, but it was nothing compared to what happened to me a few years ago.

Another afternoon of fall 2007, my bus almost destroyed the fence in the back parking lot of Candlewood Middle School. That afternoon, I left the high school with a bus almost full of students and headed south on Deer Park Road. A few seconds later, I felt that I needed to take a nap. But I fought that desire back until I finished the high school run.

After the post-trip, my best reaction would have been to park the bus in a quiet place and take a five—to ten—minute nap. On the contrary, I decided to continue to drive until I got to the middle school. When I got there, I entered my spot number. In order to park correctly between the two others buses, I backed up a few feet. To control the back of the bus and prevent any accident, I gazed at the dome mirror. As soon as I raised my head, it tilted to the back. I lost control over the muscle that controls my neck. I lost control of myself. My eyes closed, and I felt asleep.

The bus was moving back, and I could hear the backup alarm beeping the same way I could hear myself snoring when I am about to fall asleep. For a fraction of a minute, I was unconscious behind the steering wheel. Suddenly, I woke up. Surprised, I covered the brake pedals so hard that any witness standing outside could notice the bus shaking violently under the force of reaction of the brakes.

I looked forward and noticed a long distance separated the other buses from mine. I shifted back to drive and moved to my spot. Suspicious, I glanced at the Asian driver sitting on the bus next to me. He did not even stare at me, unaware of what was going on: For a fraction of a minute, the bus was my bed.

CHAPTER XV

Being A Substitute
Or A Spare Driver

In October 2008, the operations manager had another option for me. "Roman, do you want to become a substitute driver?" she asked me. Then she added, "If you pass your run to Charly, a new driver who is still in training, you'll get forty hours and also some charters."

For a few seconds, I thoroughly considered all the advantages and disadvantages, and I replied, "OK."

Later, another driver advised me to reconsider my options and wait until after the Christmas tips, since it was December.

In the meantime, a school district bus company hired me. But I worked only one and half day for this company after considering my bills and the twenty-five-hour contract. Eventually, I resigned and decided to come back to Educational Bus Company).

I went back to the EBI the second school day of the year 2009 to work as a spare driver. At that time, I have been driving for the Company for more than four years. In fact, for being familiar with the Half Hollow Hills School district area, I accepted to become a substitute or a spare diver, knowing all the risks, the surprises, the challenges, and the consequences that this kind of duty required.

i. Our Duty

Basically, nothing differentiates a spare driver's duty from a regular driver's duty, which is to drive the students safely to any destination. Nevertheless, sometimes the duty of the spare drivers may vary. Every day, we have a new task, a new route to cover, a new place to go. In brief, we still have to lift the same stone, but we need to find a new place to put it. In other terms, our duty varies according to the spur of the moment.

Our mission requires us to be bold, prompt, and always ready to serve and to go anywhere anytime. We replace absent drivers; we have to do the routes regular drivers cannot do or do not want to do; we cover breakdowns, accidents, and any other surprises; we have to catch up on lost time and drive when some drivers decide not to come due to bad weather, family problems, vacation, oversleeping, or an unpredictable event, or when a driver forgets about the time to sign in, as it was my case on Tuesday June 15, 2010.

Our duty does not stop there. During school breaks, besides doing charters, we could move, sweep, clean, paint, wax, and wash buses. During snow days, we help the mechanics clean the yard. We also pick up parts for the shop, bring mail, do shopping, and run different other errands. On some slow days, we stay seated in the drivers' room for long hours, joking and debating on some important and universal topics.

Since the recession begins, we face from the management some rational measures, which conflict with the regulations. The odds are that, sometimes being off-duty, we perform some tasks that pay less than the regular rate. Likewise, we find ourselves, even being on-duty, in a situation to accept an hourly rate lower than our regular hourly imputation when driving students. We have been taken in by the management. On Friday July 16, 2010, I was shocked after receiving my check. Unhappy, I protested so vehemently against this situation with a manager that I had to swallow three cups of water to calm my temper down. As a matter of fact, that decision of the management contrasted with the 17NYCRR 723.1a and the 17NYCRR.10i-2 of the NYS Laws and Regulations.

a. The 17NYCRR 723.1a states, "The term on-duty time shall mean and include all time from the time the driver begins to work or is required to be in readiness to work until the time he is relieved from work and all responsibility for performing work."

b.   The 17NYCRR 723.10i-2 stipulates, "The term on duty, with regard to the driving of school buses, shall be any time spent performing duties for a motor carrier, whether or not such duties involved driving of a motor vehicle."

Our complaints does not change the managers' point of view. They are rigid and never reconsider their position.

That summer, by professional ethic, I decided to continue to work against my will. I decided to accept it instead of leaving it. For some necessary reasons, I never considered the irresponsible choice of stopping working. I will never abandon the students. What is the purpose of my job?

ii. Spare Drivers Are Between Fires On The Roads

Spare drivers found themselves between fires, where they do not know which one to approach. The fires represent the stresses and strains of the pace of life in New York, the pressures and constraints that we, school bus drivers face, in the execution of our duty. The following example explains that.

One afternoon, coming out of St. Anthony High School in South Huntington, another school bus driver harassed me three times to force me to move faster. First, on my way out of the school, a blind spot prevented me from turning left safely. The driver blew the horn; I waited until the big bus in front of me cleared the way. Now, I can see the oncoming traffic on the other lane and safely make the left turn on Wolf Hill Road. The van I was driving was lower than the bus; therefore, I had to turn left and move until it was safe to go.

The second case occurred at the intersection of three streets: Pigeon Hill Road, Old Country Road, and Wolf Hill Road. The green arrow was just lit; I had to proceed. The van driver blew the horn a second time, ignoring the fact that I had to yield to a last car that was running the red light. I continued northeast on Old Country Road.

The third time, the lights just turned green on Jericho Turnpike, the deadliest street of Long Island that year. I waited two seconds, looked left and right to make sure it was safe to turn right. He blew the horn a third time, passed me and moved to the left lane to his destination. I felt upset because my aggressor was another school bus driver, but I kept myself from reacting immediately.

The next day, this driver parked behind me at the school. I walked to his bus to talk to him. I said, "How're you doing?"

"I'm fine," he responded.

"I'm Roman. What's your name?"

"Jeter."

I tried to be kind and conciliate. I looked at him straight in the face; and carefully, to avoid any confrontation, I said, "You know that you blew the horn three times behind me yesterday. First, coming out of the school, there was a blind spot because at the same time, a large bus was about to make a right, and—"

"I'm so sorry. I was in a rush. They only give me fifteen minutes to do the run, and after I've to do another school." That was his excuse.

"Do you know you'll be the first one who will be blamed, prosecuted, or punished? Do you know you'll be the first on to be hanged if something happens?"

"Sorry, man."

Sorry, easy word.

A simple oversight or the need to comply with the pressures of the roads can put us in situation where we will have to apologize for our mistakes. When we cause a disaster, a preventable accident, or an atrocious incident, we put ourselves in an embarrassing position, where we will have to beg a judge's pardon, although real and nonbiased justice is not based on pardon. We will face the consequences of our inconsequence, since our indifference has trapped us and we will be burned in the fire we have set consequently to the reality of the roads.

iii. The Reality on the Roads

The reality on the roads makes it sometimes difficult for substitute drivers to behave correctly on the roads. For being in delicate situations, we, substitute school bus drivers, very often react differently from regular drivers. How would we drive? What would be our reaction when a dispatcher asks us "to bring a bus right away and switch it with another broken one, or jump on a bus and go to do an emergency pickup?" How would we drive a bus to another driver who was already late more than fifteen, twenty minutes?

How would the managers react in case we keep being too late, or, let's say it clear, in case we move too slow? What would be the district's reaction? Two questions that only the direct antagonists, such as the dispatchers and managers, the districts employees, and the drivers, can answer. Each one faced a direct pressure from another branch of the system: district employees from school officials or opulent and influential parents, dispatchers from the district employees, and drivers from the dispatchers. Our judgment and our professionalism would dictate us how to act behind the steering wheel. The pressures and the demand of the moment can force us to move a little faster—the same happens when a police or a firefighter rushes to get to a scene of an accident or a disaster as long as we do not comply to the exigencies of the moment in a way that it gains control of us instead of us gaining control over the vehicles, over the roads, and most importantly over ourselves.

We have the choice to please the people in a rush or to protect our passengers and ourselves.

iv. Standby

Some other days, we were on *standby*. In reality, we had nothing to do. We just drove the bus somewhere; and we sat down reading a paper, talking on the phone, or watching the people in the streets, etc. These were the better days. We somehow felt we do less than what we are paid for or we got paid for doing nothing.

Here we go! On November 12, 2009, around 7:20 a.m., a dispatcher just called me while I was sitting on the North Service Road reading a paper. A female celestial voice tore the air inside the bus. "Kings Park Base to bus 1033, Roman."

"Go ahead," I replied.

"Can you bring the bus to Carl? His bus broke down on High Pasture Road."

The message was not clear.

"Say again, Carole," I asked.

Another driver told me, "High Pasture. It's a street off Melrose Road."
"OK."

I know Melrose Road. Immediately, I figured it out. I was parked in the vicinity around five minutes from that street.

When I got the call, in a fraction of a minute, I was ready to leave. Right away, I placed my bag behind the driver's seat. I rushed to the destination. I was on the first lane of the 495 Long Island Expressway; I felt the bus moving to the shoulder, and I immediately understood that this reaction was due to a high pressure zone created by a large vehicle that was about to pass me.

I held the steering wheel firmly with both hands. Indeed, a cautious glance at the left mirrors let me perceive an eighteen-wheeler. I got off at Exit 51. All the cars around me were racing to pass. As the lights on Deer Park Road were green, they did not want to miss the intersection, and I didn't either. I looked at the dashboard; the needle was pointing on fifty-five miles per hour, although the required speed limit on the Service Road is forty.

I checked the mirrors again, and on the right lane, a red sports car rushed to pass the bus because the right lane was about to end. I released the accelerator to let it pass. Now, due to the traffic, the car stopped parallel to me. I looked at the driver; and with my right hand, I pushed the air down, creating invisible waves meaning, "Take it easy! Slow down! Trò prese pa fè jou louvri (Do not rush the life)." The driver of the red sports car then went right in front of me as usual, leaving only a few feet of distance. I moved immediately to the right. Anyway, I had to make a right and went down Half Hollow Road. The lights were yellow for a long time. I passed and looked at the mirror; they became red.

Dispatch called me again. "Roman, check the bus. If you can, bring it back to the base."

Carl, the regular driver, responded, "The door is completely broken. Roman won't be able to drive the bus like that."

I continued my way until I reached the destination. The students boarded the bus; Carl followed them. I got off my bus and walked to the broken bus.

That morning, I met some students that I used to drive to Signal Hill Elementary. They treated me like a movie star. Their enthusiastic welcome lifted my spirit and let me understand how important I was for them. It doubled my conviction to continue my task in the sense of good.

I waited on the broken bus until the mechanic truck arrived a few minutes later. I crossed the street to go to the other bus. The right entrance door was titling on the side. The mechanic had to tie it with a rope so I could drive it back to the yard.

v. Risk on the Job

Very often, as substitute drivers, we found ourselves in difficult situations where we were about to have an accident. Generally, the imperfections of the left-and—rights or other parameters can likely cause us to run behind schedule. Therefore, the need to finish a run in a reasonable time keeps all our attention on the run and makes us forget about the reality on the roads.

As a matter of fact, one afternoon, I covered a route in Hicksville. From Broadway, I turned right on East Marie St., with my left hand holding the steering wheel, my eyes on the roads and the left-and-right paper in my right hand. The next intersection confused me because it is shaped like a fork. I was looking for Park Avenue, but I could not read the sign. I had to turn left unless I was sure it was Park Avenue, since I was already late. The streets are narrow, and I was using a large bus, which meant it's impossible to do a U-turn.

I moved ahead without paying attention to the roads. One driver managed to pass around the front of the bus while blowing the horns. Now I realized that I had stopped in the middle of the intersection and was about to take the red light. A male driver on the left calmly waited and disagreeably glared at me probably he said, "Are you crazy?" I thought he was going to call the company; he had sufficient reason to do so, but he never did. Thanks!

vi. Other Drivers' Conception Toward Spare Drivers

Spare drivers face the wrong, erroneous, and peculiar impression of some other drivers. They bear the idea that the spare drivers' duty is simple and easy: We do nothing for the money. That is wrong!

To prove that, here is the commentary of a regular driver about me as a substitute driver. In December 2009, Alemao, a coworker entered the employees' room, approached me, smiled, and, while pouring coffee in a cup, murmured with a heavy Spanish accent, "Easy money. You just stay there watching people, and they are paying you."

I smiled while using my brain to find an answer, since I do not have this lingual spontaneity. I lack this ease to communicate, given that English is my third language (Creole is first and French, the second). I could not say a word. I did not want to say a word.

Another American spare driver replied, "Would you like to join us?"

"Naaaaa. I have family business to take care of. I have to babysit children."

That is the preconceived idea of some other bus drivers vis—a-vis spare drivers. Seemingly, one can imagine that spare drivers sometimes get paid for *doing nothing*?

At first, let us consider carefully the truthfulness of this statement. Really, for a certain period of time we might not have anything to do. Therefore, what can we do with this fraction of time? Nothing; nothing other than read a paper, contemplate the steps of clouds, joke, etc. We should stay in the limits of the yard. We are not free to either dispose of this time or go anywhere we want to. This time does not belong to us. We have no control over it.

What about a regular driver who has a three-hour break after dropping off a charter? While he is getting paid, he can use this portion of time to shop, go to the library, to walk in a park, etc. According to the circular of March 26, 2010, we spare drivers cannot stay in our car but inside the driver's room in readiness to serve.

Let us go further now in our consideration. I think the company invested multimillion dollars in this business. Management has carefully thought and has considered the pros and the cons of leaving us sitting there without doing anything. Do you think that a manager would jeopardize his or her job by accepting some lazy men to wait inside a room all day, looking at the wall, talking about other employees' business, or to tease some peaceful, faithful, and efficient workers, or even to sleep? Is there any management system that would just grant us a check for doing nothing? Is anything free in this world? I am not sure. It is the give-and-take, a bronze and an economic law that is as old as the world, where everything is based on profit. Therefore, why so many spare drivers?

The structure of school bus transportation business makes it sensible and fragile. Some school bus companies do not establish a rigorous rule in the amount of time employees have to work. A simple arithmetic calculation lets us understand the benefit made by the company from such employees' laxness. Consequently, most of them, such as young drivers, retired workers, small business owners, housewives, etc., who do not face the same economical constraints as us, migrants, young, or some old drivers, can deliberately decide not to work a day for no apparent or real reason. That is why the management needs so many spare drivers.

Some busy days, we have been solicited for different runs; and I even witnessed dispatchers, mechanics, managers go on the roads. It is also a way to diminish any employee's chance to work overtime, meaning a less concentration of salary to a group of drivers. Probably, the company increases the number to comply with the restrictions of the law and prevent us from exceeding the maximum driving time: ten hours within a period of fifteen consecutive hours (17NYCRR 723.10g, NYS Laws and Regulations 2011, p.76). By hiring more people, the company also directly helps the American government and, at the same time, obtains a better compensation. Isn't that a rational choice?

In reality, no noticeable distinction exists between a regular bus driver and a substitute driver. We just represent two links of the chain. In order to solidify it, we need to join our elbows to show great solidarity, be on the same wavelength in our decisions, and look in the direction of the sun. People and even many other drivers have to change their mind about the cliché they have heard about spare drivers' duty. Contrary to the trend, our mission is to contribute to the expansion of the company in fulfilling this noble task: ensure safely the transportation of the American students to any destination.

CHAPTER XVI

Effects Of The School Bus On Our Health

We drivers live inside the bus during a great portion of the day. In order to be used efficiently and safely, it needs to be perfectly maintained by the mechanics and kept in ideal and salubrious conditions by us. Otherwise, the effects and the consequences on our health might be disastrous. The air we breathe inside the bus, the cleanliness of the environment, body deformity due to fabricant defects, augmentation of the belly, and feeling of discomfort when running over a bump represent many cases we could face.

i. Cleanliness of the Bus and the Air Inside

a) The Euphemism

One afternoon, for not having enough time after a morning run, I only cleaned the bus from the middle to the front, leaving the back dirty. The bus was almost full of its content. When I was about to leave the elementary school, I glanced at the dome mirror and saw a little girl, the oldest of three sisters, walking in the aisle toward me. She stopped in front of me, with her right index finger pointed in my direction; she stared at me and then asked curiously, "Is this our bus, Roman?"

Feeling embarrassed, I responded, "Sorry. I forgot to sweep the bus this morning. I didn't have time."

That third grade student pertinently knew she was on the right bus, whose number was visible inside, outside, and on the top. Moreover, inside was a sticker, posted on top of the dashboard next to the radio, with my name "Roman."

Purposely, she warned me, her driver, about the insalubrious conditions inside. She deliberately used a sort of euphemism to ask me the question. I love her! She was a smart, polite, gentle, subtle, cautious, and reserved girl who, at her age, had the magic to delight, appreciate, and make us feel good while giving us an order. She was in the category of people who can make us understand that "I hate you" means "I love you." That is how wonderful she was.

b) Cleanliness

In fact, as a regular school bus driver, I kept my bus clean and presentable; I swept the floor and wiped the dash and the windows very often. Therefore, I opted to breathe and swallow a tiny portion of the dust blown by the heaters, the defrosters, or the air conditioning. As a substitute school bus driver, I have had the misfortune to cover some routes and use some buses that were in conditions so insane that I was frightened to think that a human could work in this degree of dirtiness. I had the choice either to clean it during the pretrip if there was enough time or to drive it as it was.

I also drove some buses that have been kept in perfect hygienic conditions. I would feel guilty if I did not clean them after being used. Consciously, my school bus wasn't the cleanest one in the yard. Maybe Pedro or Cyalita deserved the trophy, but I did my best to protect my students and myself.

A clean bus diminishes the chance of developing serious health concerns the rest of our life. It is in our advantage to keep it clean, contrary to what some others drivers think. To prove that, let me share with you dear reader a particular case that shows a driver's negligence regarding the care of her passengers. In June 2009, after the morning run, I entered a coworker's bus. I scanned around the dashboard and made a quick glance in the aisle; dirty seatbelts and garbage were on the floor. She invited me to sit down. I refused categorically because the bus was too filthy. Calmly, I told her, "Do you drive goats or people? C'mon! You have to clean the bus."

"Why?"

"Because it's so dirty," I replied.

The dashboard was covered with a thick layer of dirt. She continued vehemently, "I don't have time. I'm not going to clean the bus for the company and the students. You spare drivers are sitting here doing nothing. You should clean it!"

I stopped speaking. I chose not to reply.

Sadly, that driver was part of the ones who deliberately refused to clean their filthy and stinky buses. When the sun is high, those buses let escape the unpleasant smell of the seats, garbage cans, the odor of cigarettes, or all disagreeable and strong odor of sweat or other rudimentary human needs. Pardon me for relating such rudeness. Though sorry it is the truth!

In INAGHEI (National Institute of Administration Management and International High Studies), my ecology teacher used to say, "Tout se tient (It all holds together)." This meets the give-and-take law of Dr. Jean Price Mars, "who stipulates that life is impossible without an internal reaction to external influences, that the maximum adaptation of an organism to its surroundings is the greatest capacity of its malleability and resistance to the forces of annihilation; that in the end, an equilibrium, a harmony, a sort of biological mimesis is established between creature and environment." This sentence explains the natural instinct of survival of species which find themselves in difficult situation. Their progeny will find way to survive; their system will adapt to the environment.

As a matter of fact, I had to learn to adapt myself to that environment. Although in my mind, I said, "Does her kind of judgment bear any logical sense? Or is it selfishness or ignorance? Would she rather destroy her lungs than wiping up the dashboard? Come on! Does she belong to this category of people who spend all their life blaming other people for their miserable living conditions?" I do not deny the fact that some people become inherited after being stripped of everything by their oppressors; others fail in a society because they are led by unconscious, irresponsible, and greedy politicians who let misery prevail.

Dear colleagues, the time now is to learn to reason in a positive way. What do the students and the company have to do with us keeping the bus clean? We do not clean the bus for the company which is, first and foremost, an imaginary person, an economic entity. We do not clean the bus for the boss. But even if the 17 NYCRR 721.4A11 said that "we shall keep the passenger section in a clean sanitary condition," in reality, we do not clean our bus for the students. Do we clean our room for our boyfriend or girlfriend? Hope not! We clean it for ourselves. Any bus in insanitary conditions poses serious health effects for all its occupants, either driver or students. How many hours do we spend on the bus? Seven, eight, nine, sometimes ten hours; we spend our life on the bus. Isn't it also harmful for us and for our students? The students spend only fifteen, ten, five minutes on the bus. Who has every chance to be sick? Probably the driver. Some students might also be affected due to our negligence or our wickedness. Are we proud? If we are, just consider us a cynical.

c) The Environment

The yard is located in an industrial area surrounded by construction yards, recycle, and concrete companies. During wintertime, the sand used to melt the snow and dropped by the different occupants of the bus, causing its floor to be dusty; the burning of the residential wastes, the dung or other landscaping products let escape some strange smells, which consequently change the air quality we breathe. In the yard, in the schools we, school bus drivers, should know and be conscious that we are very often in situation to breathe unclean air.

In the yard, I used to be the early guy on Tuesdays (every day, one spare driver begins to work at 5:00 a.m.). The last week of December 2009, I had to check the availability of all the buses in the yard. Since it was cold, the mechanics had to start some buses. In the space of a few minutes, I found myself surrounded by smoke exhaust and other components of carbon. In the 2010 refresher, with the need to improve the air quality in the environment, a safety instructor was talking about new and preventives dispositions where we have to pretrip some portions of the bus without idling it.

In some schools, the buses are parked bumper to bumper, so we are forced to breathe a portion of the diesel exhaust that smells vinegar and escapes from the muffler of the bus in front. No choice. Frankly, after a full day of driving, I even exhaled the same gas as the bus.

What kind of gas do the people who live around inhale? Let me share with you, dear readers, an event that occurred on the bus on Monday, December 13, 2009. That morning, after completing the pretrip inspection, I parked the bus across from the office. The company just published the "5 minutes idle" rule. I run to get my bag from my car. I just stayed approximately two minutes fixing some papers, and then I went back to the bus.

To my surprise, I met Kenzo, a resident who wanted to shut the bus off, inside. When he saw me coming, he walked out of the bus.

"What are you doing here?" I asked him.

"You leave the bus on in front of my windows, and all the exhaust comes straight inside my house. I was about to shut it off."

"You know you are not supposed to enter the bus. I just parked there for one minute. I'm leaving now."

"Thanks! I really appreciate that."

"OK."

d) Body Deformity Due to Fabricant Defects

Driving a school bus can lead to many consequences in our body.

1. Spinal Structure

First, the structure of our spinal column may change if we do not sit in the right posture behind the steering wheel. Some driver's seats are uncomfortable, defective, and not well adjusted; therefore, we are prone to tilt or bend ourselves in order to have some kind of equilibrium. This posture may develop overnight a form of scoliosis or lordosis.

2. Legs Tonus

Other parts of our body could be affected by manufacturing defects in the conception of the school bus. Indeed, we could feel cramp in the legs.

We even joke about our legs, assuming that the right leg is stronger than the left. Depending on the flexibility of the accelerator pedal, we have to push hard to move the bus. Any driver who has driven an old one has surely experienced this kind of difficulty. By repeating this movement a thousand times, we tend to give one leg a better muscular tonus and a better knee articulation than the other.

3. Our Whole Body Hurts

Another kind of consequence the drivers face is the painful feeling of our body over the years. After a long driving day, our articulations, our joints lost their flexibility; our whole body hurts. So I usually stand up to stretch my legs and twist my body anytime a short break allowed me to. This helps me move smoothly. Some days, we have to sit down and drive long hours, keeping our thorax in a straight position, which can have some effects on our back.

4. Back Pain

The next consequence is back pain. We do not have to be a medical doctor to know that the human body is a strong structure, though after a full day of driving, I usually feel pain in my back the next morning.

The pain is a direct consequence of all the jolts, pressures, twists, road shock, wrong deviations, and movements our bodies have been through throughout the years. When the bus hits a bump, the tires, the shock absorbers, and other metallic components absorb a portion of the shock, while our body, most often our back, absorbs also a part of the shock. So drivers, be advised to go slowly and safely around the obstacles of the roads; or if there is no other option, decrease the speed of the bus.

5. Private

One more painful consequence is the effect on our private. One day, I drove over a bump that affected my body so badly that I felt a discomfort so intense I almost cause an accident.

Let me share with you what happened to me one morning on Commack Road. That day, I almost cried. I was going south on the right lane, passed under the bridge of the Northern Parkway. I came right in front of a pothole. Oh! Oh! It was too late for me to go around it. The lanes were very narrow, so I had no choice but to run over it. The right front tire dipped inside the hole. The impulsive force ejected me from my seat, and then I fell back on my testicles. Ahhhh! An atrocious pain pinched me right under my belly button. You are laughing, aren't you?

Since then, I always keep on the left lane anytime I am driving down Commack Road. I wish this kind of extreme and painful experience does not happen to any driver. Every man knows how painful and sensitive that body part is.

6. Our Belly

If we, as school bus drivers, or any driver, do not watch our diet, or if we neglect ourselves, we can develop a belly. I hope people do not interpret my opinion wrongly.

In fact, we sit down to drive; and consequently, we do not burn enough calories. In general, is it normal to any driver to become fat and develop a big belly? Question of choice! I'm not going to speculate in this matter. But let me say only that if we drive a bus, we need to be in good health; being in good health requires us to exercise. If we can exercise, we might have a normal stomach. It's a private matter; we are responsible for our body.

7. Defective Vision

The last consequence on our body is a defective vision. Driving a school bus, focusing our eyes on the roads, and keeping them moving can be responsible for a decrease in our vision. So the next time you ride a bus, take a little time to observe the driver's eyes. The glare of oncoming vehicles' lights or the sunlight hits us straight on the face; the reflection of the sun in the mirrors not only increases our chance to have an accident but also creates some negative effects for our vision. Any incoming car or truck with high beam or multiple lights on can be fatal to us and our passengers because they diminish our vision's field, and once we cannot see very well, we could have an accident leading to our dismissal.

A school bus driver, as any other drivers, should be in position to see any mobile or immobile object on the roads.

On the other hand, school bus drivers have also heard things they were not supposed to hear, things that upset them, and also things that leave a bad taste in their mouth. This is the subject of the next chapter.

CHAPTER XVII

Words I Have Heard

The atmosphere inside the bus is sometimes tense, sometimes smooth, and sometimes hot. Depending on the moment, the students are standing up or sitting down. Usually in the afternoon, after a long day of hard work at school, the school bus represents the ideal place for them to empty their stomach. Curses, expressions of sexual contents, funny words or gestures to distract the other students and also the bus driver, curious questions asked to the bus driver, and words or acts of discrimination occupy their state of mind for the moment.

i. The Catholic Schoolboy

It was a cold and dark morning. I waited for more than two minutes to pick up the last student and bring him to a catholic school. He did not come. I was about to pull up when another boy inside said, "Wait! He's coming."

I stopped. The other student came on the bus. The boy inside said, "I save your ass."

He responded, "Uh."

"I saw you in the corner of my eyes."

ii. Six-year-Old Teenager

One afternoon of December 2009, Carmelo, the dispatcher, entered the driver's room. He felt embarrassed to decide which driver had to do an emergency pick up to JEA Alternative School. In this case, he brought five pieces of paper containing numbers ranging from one to five, which each one of the five available drivers had to choose. I chose number three, which coincided with the one selected by Carmelo. Therefore, I had to do the run.

The dispatcher said, while handing to me the paperwork containing the student's name and address, "I need you to cover this JEA Alternative's run right away."

"OK."

He told me the van number I have to drive. Quickly, I did the pretrip; and in five minutes, I left the yard.

In less than thirty minutes, I arrived at the school. I opened the van door. A teacher came by the van; he held a walkie-talkie. "He'll be right out," he said to me.

"OK," I responded.

In a fraction of a minute, another teacher accompanied a short skinny boy to the van. He was wearing a white T-shirt and holding his jacket and his backpack in his hands in the 30 degree F temperature.

He came on the bus. "How you doing?" he said.

"All right," I replied.

I left the school. A minute later, he said to me with a mean face, "These guys don't know how old I'm." Then he continued, staring at me, "They treat me like a six-year-old boy. Do you know how old I'm?"

"I'm sorry."

"Do you know how old I'm?"

I did not stare at him too much. At first, his size and his face made him appear to be nine, or ten years old. So I imagined. "Uhhh! You might be ten, or eleven years old."

"Nooo. I'm fourteen. I'm a ninth grader. They took me off the bus because I was arguing with a bus driver who asked me to shut up."

The boy continued, "I told him don't ask me to shut up. You shut up!"

"But why?" I replied.

"Because I was fighting with a six-feet-tall boy."

Is a bus driver allowed to ask a child to shut up? It depends. I never did. Did the boy build a story? It could be, as some children do.

He sat behind me, his new bus driver at that time. One could imagine that I had to question him cautiously, balance, and measure each word before I said something. I feared he could be angry at me. I did not want to receive a blow in case he hid a weapon or a baseball bat in his backpack; I also feared being hit with his hands, because we were the only two people on the bus, and he was sitting right behind me.

He did not give me the reason he was fighting with the other student. I did not ask him for the reason either. But I suggested, "Is he bigger than you?"

He replied, "Man, it's not about big or small in this world. It's about respect. You should respect me. If you don't, I f…k you up!"

Right! He deserved to be respected as any human being should be.

Does his statement bear a bit of truth?

Years ago, when I was a teenager, a brawl between two friends did not last forever. I fought with someone, he beat me or I beat him; that was it! The brawl was over, and later, we became friends. Now, the fight will last until one of us die. Now the laisser-faire, the lack of rigor in the principles makes the world different and dangerous.

To complete this student's statement, it is not about a dangerous world. It is not about strong or weak, powerful or unknown, it is about who acts faster, who hits more violently; it is about our connections to the killers, mobs, and the dark forces of the environment.

His house was located at about one mile from the school. I drove down his street; and then he asked me, "Can you go faster? I had to run to work." Students always ask us to drive faster. It's fun. Even some teachers have the tendency to indirectly force us to move faster. Nevertheless, behind the steering wheel, we have the control; we decide. Calmly, I responded. "Don't worry. You'll be home soon."

"What street is this?" he added.

"Jackson Road."

At the next corner, he asked me, "Can you drop me off here?"

"No. I have to drop you off at your address."

A few feet later, he told me, "Stop right here."

He got off. I waited until he crossed the street, and then he entered home.

I waited a few minutes to write down this event. Two or three minutes later, he passed in front of the van, holding his jacket; he was going to work.

iii. Curious Questions

On Monday December 21, 2009, I covered a route for the Half Hollow hills School district. One male student, entering the bus, asked me. "Are you Jude?"

"No. My name is Roman," I responded.

"Woman," he smiled.

I said, "No. Not Woman. Roman."

"Ah! OK."

As a Creole- and French-speaking Haitian, I always have trouble pronouncing the letter r in English. People hear it or pronounce it differently than the way I do.

That student wanted just to tease me, since he knew his previous driver's face, another Haitian bus driver that everyone loved. Later I will tell you about him (Ref p.187).

In the afternoon, the students were getting crazy. They were horse playing, walking in the aisle, screaming, etc. Quietly, I said, "Sit down, students. We are going to leave."

On Wolf Hill Road, while I was driving, they kept fighting. To one girl who sat in the middle I said, "Lady, sit down please."

To tease or to correct me, another repeated, "Lady, sit down please."

One boy just dropped all his body on another girl. A troubled atmosphere reigned inside the bus, making it difficult for me to concentrate and stay focused on the road. I looked through the mirror, and pointing to the camera, I warned them. "Excuse me, guys. For your information, this is a camera. I can just push the red button and record everything you do."

Immediately, the students stopped teasing each other. I did the run quietly and dropped the students off. While I was going to the last stop, one of the four students on board came near me and said, "Do you like this route?"

"It's a pretty decent route," I responded.

"You know. We just got crazy sometimes."

"Come on! I get you. I was a boy too."

iv. The Little Ones

Most of the time we, school bus drivers, are in contact with children. By curiosity, the elementary students would ask us all kinds of funny, strange, and bizarre questions. Therefore, let us be ready to answer them.

Some questions came naturally from the inside; other questions sometimes have been heard from their parents or other acquaintances. One morning one boy asked me, "Bus driver, why are you always dressed up?"

I smiled.

A second one told me, "I love your cologne, Roman. I love your boots."

Thank you.

One girl added, "Are you going out after?"

Another one, getting on the bus, holding the right handrail, came up, then stopped by in front of me, looked straight at me and said, "Bus driver, why are you always wearing hat?"

I responded, "It's cold. You know, I came from Haiti. It's always hot there. I don't have a strong immune system. I don't want to have a runny nose."

I tried to find all sort of excuses. Then I took my hat off. One of them said, "Look! Roman is bold."

Another morning of December 2, 2009, I covered a Copiague route. While the children were on the bus, I looked at them through the dome mirror. I said, "Do you like school?"

One girl responded, "Yes, I love school. I love my teacher."

Another boy sitting next to her said, "School is fat."

I wanted to answer, "What kind of diet does school follow?"

Some students do their homework on the bus. One day a debate took place inside the bus, where I had to answer some math and science questions.

A bus driver should be ready to listen to all kinds of incomprehensive, difficult, and funny questions asked usually by the little students. Be attentive. If we understand them, find an answer. If not, at least smile!

v. The Principal

At 9:00 a.m., I entered the elementary school, parked, and secured the bus. As usual, almost all the students got off their seats. The principal, Mr. F. K. Rogamaneus, entered the bus. With a soft-spoken tone, he told me, "You reported Jack and Jelly yesterday."

"Yes," I replied.

"You know that anytime you report a child, it rebounds on my shoulder.

I'm the one between you and the child."

"But I have to—"

"I understand you. Remember we have to work together."

The principal was trying to convince me to use all the tangents before considering the option of reporting a child. We have two different views of the reality and use two different approaches to deal with the children. Even if we do not see them the same way, our basic objective should contribute to their well-being.

For sure, this principal was under a lot of pressure from the parents. Thus, he should manage in a way to keep his job and satisfy the demands of some influential parents.

vi. Angel's Dream

On Tuesday, January 22, 2008, the day after Martin Luther King's birthday, during a late activity from Forest Park Elementary School, I witnessed a student's testimony. The previous year, I drove these students who, somehow were good, but often went crazy. Above all, most of them attended elementary school for their last year before going to middle school.

For some students, the bus represented the ideal place to discharge all kinds of vulgar comments, to talk about some delicate topics, and to debate about their observation in life. In fact, one tall and skinny boy made a comment about peanut butter and jelly. He pronounced it in a way to entertain the other children. Another kid joked about something else. Each one was trying to enjoy the moment his own way. Though a little boy, usually quiet, struck my attention when he began to repeat some words the famous Dr Martin L. King pronounced in his speech from the steps of the Lincoln Memorial, "I have a dream." Among what he said, I could remember:

"I have a dream. I have a dream the cafeteria will only serve fried chicken, pizza and pepperoni.

I have a dream that people will have no money.

I have a dream that people will have no job.

I have a dream that America will have no power, no war."

Anyone reading these lines might say, "Get out of here! You've made this story. You're so funny."

Though I am one hundred percent sincere, those are the words that came from a child's mouth, an innocent boy, a prophet. Words full of meaning, words full of consequences. An Haitian quote states, "Ti moun'n se ti zanj. (Little kids are little angels.)"

There might have been many good reasons why he pronounced these famous words. Maybe he did an essay in school, or last night, he watched a movie where the protagonist repeated the speech, or he walked in a parade where he had heard these words. Maybe he remembered the message of his pastor in the church. Maybe he was in a play in honor of this great man.

Now let us analyze the contents of each sentence to reveal the hidden truth behind each one of them.

a) I have a dream the cafeteria will only serve fried chicken, pizza and pepperoni.

No one ignores the effect of a piece of fried chicken, or the wonderful effect of a slice of pizza on our tasty papilla. As a Haitian child, I took good pleasure when it was time for dinner. Who does not like those kinds of fried, oily, and tasty meals even when the consequences could be sometimes hurtful for our health? After all we always say, "If it doesn't kill us, it will make us stronger" (Friedrich W. Nietzsche).

Let us dare suppose that he thought for his stomach. Nevertheless, he had also another perception of the reality in the second dream.

b) I have a dream that people won't have either jobs or money.

This particular child is endowed with a sixth sense. Can a ten or eleven-year-old boy predict the future? At that time, they were talking about "Stimulus of the Economy." Or was he living the worst period in his life at home? Perhaps, with that period of recession, where the capacity of buying for the household was reduced significantly due to lack of job, and, ipso facto, lack of money, that was his way to forecast the early warning signs of social and economical problems in America. Was this little angel in measure to analyze the bad conditions of existence the American people were going through at that time? I forget the author who said, "The worst conditions of existence make often the human noblest tendencies to manifest." Did this child understand that many elderly people have to work often not because they want to stay active (as some of them pretend), but because they had no other choice than working to survive until they can't? Come on! It's a dead end, no other way out. The indexation of their pensions represents nothing compared with the complex reality of the market, making it virtually impossible for them to survive with such little allocations.

Did he see a disaster coming? Here is his third dream that evening:

c) I have a dream that America will have no power, no war.

Mmm! *No power*, this is a big phrase. When talking about political and economical power, the first country that comes in our mind is the USA. No power for America. Was this statement heresy or truth; fiction or reality? What about the Roman's warning, "Si vis pacem para bellum"? (If you need peace prepare war). Did this boy understand the principle of historic determinist? Why does he have to think like that? Can he outlook the political and economic American future to see how gloomy it is? Can he see through the reality of the moment to go beyond it?

Furthermore he said, "No war." Either he was aware of thousands of warriors and innocent people, who died every year, or one of his family member was a victim of war, or he has watched such atrocities on television. Probably he was also a vector of peace following the same current of thought as Martin L. King who once said, "Do you know a good war or a bad peace?"

This boy was not the only one dreaming; drivers also dream.

vii. Driver's Dream

It was a quiet morning; many spare drivers and drivers' assistants filled the employees' room. Most of the time, we spoke about all kinds of topics, some more fascinating than others.

In general, when reading the paper, one of us always brought up a subject for discussion. Sometimes we talked about Voodoo in Haiti, sexual harassment, war, homosexuality, sex addiction, bible, religion, etc. Almost every day, an interesting plea about a topic took place among some drivers. Indeed, that morning, a particular one caught my attention: becoming rich by playing lotto.

The drivers talked about many people who have won the lotto and became poor a few years after. Some even considered themselves winning one day. What a wonderful dream!

I had the impression that they were sleeping and dreaming with their feet on earth and their eyes open. They wondered about what they would do with the money in case a happy situation like that happens.

One driver fantasized. "If I became rich, I would do a will to my family and enjoy the rest of my wealth."

A second one, the tallest among them, said, "I would stay silent, and I would take my time to know what to do with the money. I would move to another town. I would change my phone number to eliminate any contact with anybody because so many are going to come after me in search of a kind of favor. I would stay away from the crowd. Then I would find a good accountant. And finally at the end of the year, I would help my family."

Probably they would do other things with the money. Some would change their face to become younger or more attractive; others would fix their nose, change their teeth, extend their hair, implant new hair if they are bald, reduce their abdomen, or increase the size of their breasts or their buttock, etc. So many interesting things they could do with this easy money.

I don't want it!

Everyone in this world has his fantasies, his passions, and his dreams. As far as I am concerned, I have mine. Therefore, it is not my concern to censure people for playing lotto. Do not interpret my observation wrongly. As it is their private life, what is important for me is to not feel my heart racing on my chest faster than normal when I am getting the results.

To be clear, I think it is a question of faith. Obviously, people may believe they can win the lotto. Personally, I am not living for this thing. After all the pressure that I am enduring in this life, I am not going to add more on my burden.

Briefly, I am not going to play a game when I know that the chance to win six numbers successively tend to zero. When people are drowning, they hang themselves on to all the branches (La Vi Nou Yòk, Theodore Beaubrun, Languichat Debordus).

CHAPTER XVIII

Bad Words And Expressions Of Sexual Contents

i. The Clown

During my first year as a bus driver, I drove a funny boy from West Hallow Middle School. When the atmosphere inside the bus was tense, he was the one to break it. He used to say loud, F…k me, babe! F…k me, babe!

At first sight, any analysis of the content of this phrase means that he is cursing at himself. Automatically, I translate it in my mother's language, the Creole. It gives me a funny expression that anytime I remember, or anytime I want to laugh, I try to say it to myself. How funny it is.

This student neither had any bad intention nor wanted to be hostile toward any other student on the bus. He was the clown, the darling of the girls. He said that just to break the tension inside the bus. He did it with art and great fineness, since he chose the right moment to throw the arrow. Sometimes I had to stop him when he wanted to cross the limits of morality. I remember that he used to talk about some other sensible matters such as what kind of woman he likes, the shape of buttock he enjoys; he classifies the penis size of the different human race, etc. Talking about size, this is what we share in the following lines.

ii. The Three Girls

One afternoon, the sky was getting dark; three High School East girls just entered the bus. They were standing and talking about an interesting topic. One of them, while fixing her hair, said, "Me, I'm taking a French class."

The other answered, "Me, I hate French. I'm taking Spanish instead."

The third one, a skinny petite girl, said loudly, "Neither French nor Spanish interests me. What interests me is a black man with a…"

I leave it to you, dear reader, to imagine the rest.

They all burst out loudly while their eyes met my eyes in the mirror. Then the last girl, without the least hint of embarrassment, added while looking at me, "Bus driver, do you have a big p…?"

Confused, in search for an answer, I turned my head looking at the street through the driver's window. With a calm voice and serious face, I responded, "No idea."

In situation where students seek our opinion on sensitive matters, we keep a relaxed and serious face. We do not smile; we do not comment.

iii. Sensitive Matters

No idea—right answer in an uncomfortable situation. A boy stood right in front of me, holding my chair and looking at me. With his right hand, he pointed at a girl who just got off the bus and was waiting for him at the curbside. He bent and asked me, "Bus driver, a pretty girl like that can have sex three times a day?"

I swallowed my saliva; in order to cultivate the sense of decency, I decided to stay mute. All bus drivers should keep a limit in those conversations. Those sensitive matters can put us in deep trouble. Be careful! He wasn't a regular student; it was the second time he rode the bus. He was just trying to be nice and funny, to get along with me. After that comment, he left.

iv. Inappropriate Language

Remember this when the situation crosses the limit, we have to intervene. I intervened one day at the beginning of 2008. One turbulent boy opened the bus window and loudly shouted to a girl who just left the bus, "Can you have sex with me?"

The girl did not even look back. At his stop, on his way out of the bus, I raised my right hand to draw his attention and said, "You're not allowed to say anything you want on the bus."

He responded, "Sorry, bus driver. I'm going to be good."

The abovementioned examples show that sex is a hot topic discussed inside the school bus. Dennis Walcott, the New York City Chancellor, is aware of the reality of "sex between students before the age of thirteen, students who have multiple sexual partners, and students who aren't protecting themselves against sexually transmitted diseases and HIV/AIDS." That is why, Yoav Gonen, a New York Post education reporter commented on that article, "The Chancellor sent a carefully worded e-mail to all middle school and high school principals informing them that they no longer have a choice about whether they want their students to learn such things as how to put on condoms and the danger of sexual promiscuity." Thus, for a good cause, he stated, "City school will have to start teaching sex education to their students again—that's an order" (New York Post, August 10, 2011).

Surprisingly, not only students use inappropriate language on the bus.

School bus drivers also forget to speak with the voice of reason, or sometimes curse. Some of us have been blamed, reported, or even fired as a result of deliberate speech. To corroborate my point about the lack of decency in the dialogue inside the bus, a new school bus driver's commentary caught my attention. In fact, being new on the job, he had to ride the bus with me every day until he became familiar with the route he was supposed to do.

Along the roads, we met joggers, bikers, and women walking their dogs. All of a sudden, we passed a fitted pretty petite woman walking her dog on Melrose Road. He pointed his finger in her direction and commented, "That's b…s…A woman does not have to walk her dog in the street. At home, I opened the door and let my dogs shit in the backyard. After, I pick it up."

Then he gave me a look of complicity and added, "A woman doesn't have to exercise in the morning after a good night of sex."

v. Curses

After seven years in the job, I have realized that some words like f…, s…, b…, n…, etc., are embedded in the American language; the children used them automatically for fun.

As a proof, one morning I was picking up the elementary school students; the bus contained already half of its content. One of the students, a four or a five grader boy, who came by my seat and almost crying, begged me, "Bus driver, I forget my instrument. Can you go back home with me?"

I responded, "Fine."

I turned around and stopped in front of his house; the boy got off the bus. While he was walking in the sidewalk, another boy teased him. "F…k you!"

I got off my seat, walked back in the aisle. I told him, "If you have no minimal respect for the other students, you don't respect yourself either. That's why you adopt this kind of speech on the bus."

He looked at me and then bent his head down. I tried to convince him not to adopt this kind of speech; I explained to him that he might be in the company of important people. He might, without realizing it, commit the mistake to speak dirty. Based on a wrong and biased impression he had given, and as a result of an erroneous preconception, people are going to judge him in terms of his language.

Ironically, that day, I also made a big mistake. In fact, here's what came from me, Roman, the bus driver, while I was advising the boy who just cursed his friend: "If you are having a conversation with the President of the USA, are going to use the same s…?"

"Oops!" I covered my mouth.

I have made a mistake; I apologized immediately to the students. They never said a word. They did not care.

Children learn by example. They usually take up their parents' manners, their accents. They tend to walk, sigh, and move almost like them.

That is why bus drivers should be wary of saying what they want. We have to use a reserved speech; we should practice the sense of decency and not keep an offhand manner, prevent any disruptive and antisocial example. All school bus drivers should force themselves to be of exemplary behavior, a good model for the children. Even if the students spend a little time, an hour or more on the bus, our good behavior, our comportment would not change them completely but would make a little difference. Most often, children like to imitate. Let us, school bus drivers, give them a reason to talk, move, act, etc., the same way we bus drivers do. Let us act courteously, so our riders follow our path for their well-being.

vi. Victim of Indifference

I just picked up three students at 10:35 a.m. I had to wait for two more to come; though one inside the bus, a boy, told me, "That's it! You can go now."

I smiled and replied, "Not yet!"

After two minutes, the two other students came in.

The unexpected actions of these students categorize them among the most dangerous students that exist. Some are ex-convicts; others are still in probation. In the space of a blinking, they can disturb the atmosphere inside the bus. They can act violently and spontaneously; they are capable of doing the worst things we can imagine.

Strangely, one of them, a boy, cursed loudly to draw my attention. No one answered him. He went all the way to the back, sitting in a seat opposite to a girl. He continued to empty his stomach of all sort of hideous and bestial words. One last word, one last arrow hit so hard that one stout girl, to defend herself, cursed back. The plea continued vehemently between the two students.

In order to calm the students, I asked them to stop arguing. They have not been tamed young, if you'll pardon me this expression. Indeed, they were not the kind to obey easily. In the space of a few minutes, I had no illusions that I can bring them to heel easily. So since they have been sitting, I decided not to intervene.

To face the boy's insults, suddenly the girl began to sing, to dance, and to shake her body to the lyrics and harmony of a rap music. Thus, to reply, the boy did the same gesture.

I wanted to laugh, but I said, "No, Roman!"

A virulent argument between two teenagers of opposite sex just changed the bus in a free and live show that I have enjoyed to relax my mind during the trip and, for a moment, forgotten about the world.

Can we forget these students? For sure, no. They represent a direct consequence of the abuses, indifference, negligence meanness of their parents, or a reflection of the tolerance of the American educational system. We have the impression that the system or society does not need them. They just send them to school in order to prevent them from disturbing peaceful people.

vii. Accusation of Blackness

I was surprised to hear a second grade boy saying to another black child older than him, "You are so black I can't even see a bug on you."

In reality, should we condemn a six-year-old boy for this naïve opinion? Is he responsible for this commentary or this interpretation? Or has he heard it somewhere?

Clearly, it is really difficult for a child of this age to make this kind of comparison and use these words with such a tact and concise meaning. There is every chance that he has heard it somewhere. Perhaps, he picked it up at home, at a camp, in a daycare from another child, because like all men, "he was born well, but society corrupted him" (Jean Jacques Rousseau).

CHAPTER XIX

Racial Discrimination

i. The Facts: The Cold Spring Harbor Waterfowls

During a charter to the Cold Spring Harbor Fish Hatchery, I made a strange observation. In fact, after dropping off the students, I climbed the stairs located at the south side of the parking lot and walked through the bush that gives access to the lake. Two white waterfowls were swimming along the shore in front of the church. I came closer to observe; the birds went away to deep water. By precaution, I moved back and waited in a safe place to contemplate the beauty of the lake. Two minutes later, a white couple came and stood at the same place I was. Strangely, seeing them, the waterfowls that went away from me returned along the shore with the hope of getting a piece of bread from them.

How can we interpret this?

One Haitian proverb states, "If the dog runs away when you squat to lace up your shoes, you are a bum. If not, you are a good person."

Did the waterfowls manifest what Orson Scott Card, in his book *Characters and Viewpoints*, calls the complex "of the chimpanzee who classifies the stranger, then reacts accordingly."

Before, he said, "The process we call prejudice or stereotyping can lead to embarrassing false assumptions, needless fears, and even vicious unfairness."

In this case, let us suppose it was a kind of fear. Why me? I sound funny and bizarre. In reality, prejudice is intrinsic to everyone. Orson Card continues, "It is built into our biology...Strangeness is always both attractive and repellent."

It was the first time I went there. For sure I was a stranger, but not the first black human to visit that lake.

In this context, can we interpret it as a kind of discrimination?

ii. Racial Discrimination

The world history proved that racial discrimination is a direct or indirect function of our status, of our origin, of our environment, and of many other factious parameters. My concern is not to speculate on this notion of race that is tearing the world apart. I keep a distance from the apparent cycle of differences—if, after the pigmentation one, there is any—between blacks, whites, and any other color. They have been debating this matter for years.

Evidently, inside the school bus, some acts of racial discrimination are visible and tangible. I am forced to give you an idea of the racial reality and the tension that exist inside the bus. Let me relate to you some cases I have witnessed.

iii. The Last Stop

One day, three high school boys, two whites and one black, were my last passengers on the bus. They were talking and laughing. Soon after, the black student had gotten off the bus, the taller white boy commented, "He's the whitest man I've ever seen."

This commentary gives me the impression that the black student might have been too fanatical about his white community, or too faithful to his white friends. Perhaps he just moved to the town, or maybe his parents might have been economically more secured or better educated than the other students' parents. So many reflections one can raise until we can get to the truth behind this opinion. After all, only the boy knew the motive of this remark.

iv. Black Music

What about this remark of a black girl who, during a late run, asked me, "Roman, could you turn the radio on a black station because I only listen to black music?"

I smiled and negatively moved my head. Does music have any color? Isn't it the same erroneous conception of some Haitian musicians "who don't listen to some kind of devil music?"

Given that she was a leader on the bus, I did not change the station because I did not want to grant that erroneous request, and that way, give a reason to the other black students to make the same comment in the future. For a second time, she asked me the same question, but she could not convince me to change it. She was around ten, eleven years old. Did she understand the effects and the importance of all kinds of music?

I always agreed to change the radio station anytime I have been asked to do so. Though for the first time, I decided not to change it to a black radio station, not to a new frequency.

Can a music lover choose to listen to some kinds of music? Would it be the same for an astronaut to decide to explore some specific parts of the universe? That way, the musician would never listen to some melodies and the astronaut would diminish his field of knowledge. Knowledge is like the universe. We learn more by adventuring our mind to differences. I never forget this coworker's remark: "The more we learn, the more we need to learn, and the more we realize how stupid we are."

v. My Daughter's Case

The night of May 5, 2010, my daughter explained to me, "Some white students in my high school's cafeteria were throwing garbage at me and my Haitian girlfriend. Dad, I have been confronting this problem for a long time." She continued, "I waited many days to see if it was a mistake or if they were doing it on purpose." She concluded, "Papa, these students are racist."

"OK, I'll take care of it."

Since the constraints of work and the conflicts of schedule made it difficult for me to go to the school, I called the school guidance and explained the situation to a receptionist. She referred me to Mr. Sergelus, who was not present at that time; I left a message in his voice mail. He called me, and I exposed the problem to him. Later, I asked my daughter about the situation. She told me that the other students have been moved to another table.

vi. A School Bus Driver's Comment

Anyone who lives in America has the right to question racial discrimination. Should we live for that?

One afternoon Jordao, one colleague bus driver, stepped into the employees' room. He was really upset because inside his bus, some black students were complaining about the complexity of the relation between blacks, whites, and other ethnic group in USA. He stated, "Students don't have to let this idea hunt their spirit. They have become sick." Eating a chocolate sandwich, he continued, "Why do they have to talk about racial discrimination?"

"Come on! They have to express their feelings," another Spanish driver commented.

I listened to this dialogue with a sustained attention and a passion to know. For many years, since I moved to America, I have heard black people's debates and comments about races in barber shops, between Haitian and American black friends. I never had the chance to listen to Latinoes' comments. Now let us return to this driver's conception of this dilemma.

Jordao, the driver, with an angry and threatening tone, concluded, "Their parents are responsible. They just have to *grow up* and live their life. Who knows what they are going to be tomorrow?"

Right! In order to know what we want to be tomorrow, we should try now to create a destiny, answer some important questions, and touch some compound topics. One way to understand the state of things is to learn to cultivate this natural curiosity that burns from the inside.

vii. The Indian Boy

One year, I confronted difficulties with a boy who refused a younger Indian boy to sit down next to him, although only a white fence separated their houses. Usually the first month, the school assigns a seat to each elementary student. According to the list, those two boys had to sit down next to each other on the same bench. After a few days, the older boy almost every day found something fictitious to complain about the Indian boy.

One day I told him, "Aren't you friends? You'll have to go a long way together."

Why was he complaining? Multiple reasons came in my mind such as bad faith, prejudice, hatred, selfishness, parent's order. He never stopped bothering the Indian boy until I intervened one day and indeed decided to switch the younger boy. This causes another black boy from a higher grade than them to protest, "Bus driver, he has to sit down here. This is a free country."

I smiled and whispered, "Free country." In my mind, I said, "What a shame!"

"Free country," those are two words, an expression that lacks a real meaning. One day, son, you will have to face the true American reality. You will give another interpretation to this term. That's what you call freedom. Freedom doesn't exist. Depending on our position in the social scale, we will describe and interpret it our way.

In sum racial discrimination is not innate; we become racist. We have been taught our prejudice. Even a dog can reflect his owner's fear or prejudice on another person. We learn to cultivate racism by fear or in order to hide our complex. As paradoxically as it may appear, I thank God for not being born in the USA. You are shocked, aren't you? Apparently, many people from any race who have been brought up in the USA had, at least once, faced a minimal racial friction from any other race, even from his own. As a matter of fact, according to the USA Today/Gallup poll published on August 4 2008, racism is widespread in America because 51 percent of whites, 59 percent of Hispanics, and 78 percent of blacks suffer from it. Where I come from, Haiti, racial discrimination is not a burning issue because 95 percent of the Haitian population are black.

Although rooted differences exist between races in America, we should not differentiate ourselves from any other human being whose appearance is not the same as ours. In this new world, the time now is not to raise problem, given that anyone who breathes the epidermic conflict that is raging out chains himself with problems.

Are we racists because we are convinced that we owed something? For that reason, we feel a kind of insecurity. Are we scared of the oppressed because we have been oppressors? Racism is synonym of sickness. It is a disease that touches us—a gangrene that eats into anyone facing differences, or anyone who has done something wrong. It is an imaginary and scary shadow that follows us throughout our life. It is an idea that haunts our spirit every time we remember the act. It could be remorse. Racism bears, among others, a lack of something, a desire of prevalence, an interior sentiment of guilt, a low self-esteem. Racism is a way to dominate. Racism sounds like a kind of noise we make to intimidate the prey. Are we predator?

Racism is a raucous and continuous echo of our voice that we do not want to hear.

CHAPTER XX

Things And People I Have Seen

The third key of the Smith System states, "Keep your eyes moving." Clearly, when we moved our eyes we have seen so many things under the blue sky during thousand hours of duty. In the yard, in the driver's room, on the streets, in the other cars, we have seen so many strange things and people that we were not supposed to see. We have seen things that pleased us and also things that could take our breath away. The list is long.

i. Respect of Time

The respect of time represents, among others, one of the basic elements where rests America's strength. Time, a symbol of discipline, is crucial in the application of multiple daily tasks. Every morning, we meet the same cars, the same people waiting for the bus or rushing to the bus station. Others, to catch the train, risk crossing dangerous intersections. Every day we meet the garbage truck, the mailman almost at the same time. Over the years, a rigorous observation of this routine lets us understand why any vehicle driver running one minute late can cause a lot of traffic problems.

ii. Students are Being Victims of the Fashion

Young, innocent, naive, inexperienced, crazy about love, in search of a treasure, having the need to taste the happiness, etc., female students are direct victims of the fashion industry. In the prime of their lives, they face and experiment this northern wind of adventure that crosses the path of all teenagers.

In wintertime, high school and middle school girls tend to take their jackets off and reveal the doves on their stomach. During summertime, some girls come on the bus, wearing pants, and later get off with little extremely short skirts. Why do they have to change inside the bus? They make us, without our consent, some sort of silent accomplice of their tricks. Some high school girls attract people's attention by walking in the school with pants so tight that people can read all their "classical furnitures," as my friend used to say. I ask myself if these pants do not hurt. Surprisingly, even some female coworkers give the same free show, where their casual styles do not let people guess or make out what are hiding in the distance. Hey, school bus drivers, watch out! These are dangerous distractions and fatal hazards.

Nowadays, students' nudity has been exploited in all its dimensions and in all its totality. School officials should give an alarm cry to prevent students, particularly girls, from showing private parts of their body. Female students should dress discreetly in order to stop all kinds of covetousness from pedophiles and also to stop predators and child offenders. We should hold out the prospect of a mouse to a cat. T-shirts that do not cover the girls' belly buttons and show a big part of the breasts should not be accepted; tight, skin, or *moulants* pants embroidered or printed with all kinds of erotic and attractive adjectives such as wet, sweet, tasty, etc., should be banned from the school.

A child's body is a sacred thing that needs a certain protection against the assaults of the predators. At fifteen, a girl is the spitting image of a saint with an immaculate body, a naive face, and eyes full of innocence. When she is walking, her shoulders defy gravity; all men have to turn to look at her symphonic allure. Young and in prime of her life, "she can easily fall under the charm of an English teacher," as the French singer Enrico Mathias said.

According to a United Kingdom study, the designers take pleasure in making some clothes that represent a kind of stimulus for pedophilia. Very young, the girls fall under what Naomi Wolf call, "the beauty myth where the woman is never satisfied with her beauty." The society or the designers force her, without her consent, to sell her body. Tell me, what do you think when seeing a girl wearing pants with the inscription, "Sweet or Tasty?"

Tell me sincerely! Tell me.

It is clear that parents are also responsible for this indifference toward the girls' body. And for a good reason, the American Psychological Association stated that some parents think it is cute for their daughters to wear T-shirt with inscriptions, "So many boys, so little time." It is a trickle-down effect and a trickle-up effect world. In other words, children become adults before their time, and adults do not have any embarrassment dressing like teenagers.

iii. The Right to Kiss

On my bus, students are not allowed to act or behave the way they want to. Sometimes if I notice two students sitting quietly together on a seat where I cannot even see their hair, there is every chance that something serious is happening.

When it is dark inside, we cannot have a total control over the bus. One afternoon, I had a bus full of high school students. On my way down Bagatelle Road, I raised my head and saw one boy touching a girl, who experienced such a sweet pleasure that the erotic noises she produced began to disturb me. I gave them an explanatory look, but continued on driving. I turned right on main street, Wheatley Heights, then I raised my head again. Now, the girl lied down; the boy was on top of her. Their mouth connected; they had to share a tasty candy. Without the least hint of embarrassment, they offered a free spectacle in front of the other students, who were sitting quietly as if nothing was going on. I stopped the bus to look up at them through the mirror. With a firm and severe tone, I shouted, "I'm sorry, guys, I can't drive a bus while you are kissing. I'm not a chauffeur. I'm a school bus driver."

Keeping their heads down in a sign of guilt, they did not even say a word.

However, another girl sitting in the middle of the bus protested, "What's the problem, Roman? They are just kissing."

I looked at her, but I decided not to reply for fear of raising a continuous argument on the bus with her. I just whispered, "Wow!"

iv. Moral Lesson

The Oxford dictionary defines *moral* as a characterization of something that concerns with the principles of right and wrong behavior and the goodness or badness of human character.

Moral is based on precepts established by people for people. Although our natural human character makes it sometimes difficult for us to follow them blindly, we force ourselves to act accordingly. And oftentimes, you'd think everyone who literally follows these rules would look ridiculous. Indeed, we sometimes deviate from the rules, speak inappropriately, or even act rudely. Therefore, we can be reminded or warned by others in order to keep our steps with its principles, which leads me to the following moral lesson that I have learned from a student.

In fact, to one boy who was standing on the bus I said, "Yo, sit down please!"

He looked at me from head to toes, then castigated me, "Don't call me *yo*. Am I your friend? Did we go to the same school? My name is Gerald. You should learn how to talk to people." Pointing his finger to me, he said, "Never talk to me like that."

I just shook my head and drove away to the destination. I shut my mouth. I did not respond to him. I did not fight back, for I was wrong. Perhaps he wanted to hit me. Who knows? Thank God I was fat and appeared bigger than him!

I was trying to be cool. But since then, I realize that the complex reality of life in America, the challenging task to shape students our way, and the fragile and sensible interactions with them ask us to act with measure and require us to be cool with them. Not too cool; we can get burn!

v. A Love Story

On a nice afternoon, all the school buses were parked parallel to another in the West Hallow Middle parking lot. It was 2:30 p.m. I was sitting on the bus; the crowd of students left the school building to go to their regular buses. Mine was almost full of its content; perhaps one or two students were missing. I looked at the right; two kids, a boy and a girl, were standing by the curbside. With his arms, the boy wrapped the girl's neck, giving her the comfort of his body; her silky hands resting on his back, awaking all his nerves. Their bodies shook under the icy breeze; their pink-colored mouths with the taste of sugar cane finally connected. For the day, they had to share a last, a tasty kiss. Unfortunately, it was time to go home. They forgot about everything in a world that only existed for them as if the end was nearby. I somehow felt that they thought that they were the only normal people in this crazy universe.

Suddenly, a female teacher broke them off in the middle of their act. She approached and waved to them the same way the farmer waves to chicken to prevent them from eating crops.

They looked at her.

But lost in their pleasure, they did not want to see her, because their performance was more serious, more important than going on the bus and perhaps to be subjected to the screams of an embittered, ruined, destroyed, complexed, exploited school bus driver, or to suffer the attacks, the abuses, the bullies of the other jealous students. Surely, each one fulfilled the empty part of the other. Was that the only attention each one has gotten that day? Maybe one of them did it to tease a rival, or to upset an ex.

For one last time, they looked respectfully at that female teacher, who, at least once in her life, shivered with loving fever. One final magnetic force of love connected their fresh, warm, and wet shaking lips, with the color of strawberry. They became one and indivisible. One breathed for the other: a perfect love story.

The moment came, they had to leave. Each one headed toward a particular destination with a heart full of joy. They entered their respective bus with a living memory of an act that they can't wait to dream over the night.

Now, let us come back to earth. Let them fantasize about loving. Let us talk about other things I have seen on the roads of Long Island.

vi. A Piece of Me

One afternoon, while I was driving down Old Country Road to drop off Saint Anthony High School students home, a heavy rain started to fall. I looked to the right; a soaked piece of cloth with red and blue color lied on the curb side. I looked again. "What's that?"

"A flag.

It was a piece of me, the symbol of my country. It was my flag, the Haitian flag, drowned in a lake of water at the corner of Deer Park Road and Old Country Road. I wanted to get out and pick it up. But I couldn't. I had children on board.

The flag was there looking at me. It was there waiting for me to get it off the cold water. Last night, the damp air caused it to shrink and to change position. That afternoon, it was blazed, and its color had faded under the ray of lights. Maybe one Haitian left it there; maybe it was thrown away by one among a vast number of Haitians who keep denigrating their country because they have the choice to live in the USA contrary to the others who have no other choice but to stay in Haiti; maybe it was trampled underfoot by one son of our land.

As a result, they have betrayed J. Jacques Dessalines and all the Haitian ancestors; they have dumped Catherine Flon and deflowered Haiti, the virgin.

vii. A Father's Blind Reaction

A close observation during the pickup time lets me perceive and understand the sense of sacrifice some parents go through in order to build a good and secure future for their children. The following example relates to the extent of a father's love.

Every morning, he accompanied his daughter to the bus stop. I stopped the bus; he gently greeted me. His daughter kissed him, and with the right hand, he tapped her on the left shoulder. This gesture hides a sign of tenderness, a kind of connection, an advice, a way to show her that he will be with her. By touching her, he gives her an electric shock meaning, "I love you! You are in good hands, darling. Be good!"

We feel that natural and intimate relation, that pure love, that sincere sympathy, that fluid, that harmony, a symbiosis between two people in love. As if their umbilical cords were connected. In a real family, all fathers were supposed to be like him.

I also want to be like him and be with my daughters in spite of the thousands of kilometers that separate us. One dark morning, I picked up that fragile and innocent girl that was under her father's protection; the idea of my daughters' situation crossed my mind. Sadly, I could not hold back the tears. I felt my heart tearing apart under the excess of my pain. So I turned my head. I did not want to let him see me crying. Like him, I would like to watch my daughters growing, to protect them as all fathers would do, to treat them well, to show and explain to them the good side and the dangers of life, to spend quality time with them. But the reality is otherwise. I am here; they are over there in Haiti, far from the USA where I'm living; no chance to see them grow, to observe their transformation, to contemplate their beauty, to protect them against the assaults of the predators.

Though being too caring sometimes causes our reaction to be risky and blind, and the consequences can be fatal.

In fact, that morning, I opened the door; the red lights came on, and the yellow arm came up in front of the bus. While his daughter was walking to the bus, a car driver, ignoring the flashing red lights, was rushing to pass.

As soon as the father saw the car coming, he ran in front of the bus, jumped in the middle of the street to stop the car. Indeed, he offered himself in sacrifice so that the rule of law could prevail. Fortunately, the driver who had quick reflexes and the time to go around him, passed anyway. And yet he might have killed him, pretending that he did not see him. Stunned, I sighed, thinking about his blind reaction.

Acting this way could be fatal for him. He was so flushed with anger that he became red immediately. Running in front of a car to stop it was not the right reaction. As a bus driver, I have been in situation of harassment on the roads more than a thousand times.

I understand his fear, his sense of discipline. Sometimes, it would be better to raise the hands and capitulate when we know for sure we can risk our neck. Question of strategy, isn't it?

viii. Bus Drivers Interaction: Waving

My town, Huntington Long Island, gives me a feeling of home, my native country Haiti, where there was a time people in the streets used to wave to each other when they met. In some parts of Long Island, if we pass someone in an isolated location, we courteously say good morning.

In fact, school bus drivers who meet on the roads react the same way. We wave to the other drivers either by solidarity, or by simple courtesy, or by pure automatism. We do not mind waving a thousand times to another bus driver. Is it necessary for a school bus driver to wave to another school bus driver? Not really; it is a deliberate choice. We can wave as much as we can, anytime that gesture, at that precise moment, does not encroach upon our ability to drive the bus or reduce the safety requirements. During my career driving a school bus, I observed the interactions of two particular drivers who caught my attention.

The first one was a Half Hollow Hills female driver who I often met at the intersection of Old Country and Wolf Hill Roads. For the whole year 2005, she never missed the opportunity to wave to me and give me that contagious smile. I somehow felt that she had a feeling of guilt in case she forgot to wave to me.

The other driver that I used to meet during my midday in the parking lot of Laurel Road School, Northport had no feeling of guilt. In fact, among the three other school bus drivers, he was the only one who never waved back to me; he never even looked at me. The way he kept his head straight looking ahead gave me the impression he could not move it. Although to my surprise, the first school day of the year 2007, he saluted me. Since then, he never looked at me again, as if looking at me could be a sign of surprise; or perhaps it hurts when he turned his head.

To conclude, we, school bus drivers, wave to each other to symbolize our pride in doing a noble job. To show respect to the others, we wave. We wave to appreciate anything good that other drivers have done for us. We, school bus drivers, wave to each other to show our sense of duty to the community. We wave to parents to appreciate their kindness, their support, their solidarity. Sometimes we even wave to strangers for their comprehension, for their patience in helping us stay out of trouble during the loading and unloading time. We wave to make somebody else happy. We also wave to convince those who don't want to wave to begin to do so. Finally, we wave with two fingers open to show that we are on the side of peace, or we want to take part in the "coumbite of peace" that the world is craving for.

ix. The Symbol of Peace

In September 2009, the first school day, a driver lost his regular route as a result of an incident that happened in the elementary school. Therefore, as a spare driver, I covered the route. That morning, I entered Legends Court to pick up the elementary students and stopped in front of each stop as required by the school district. After each stop, the number of children increased more and more. At the same time, the atmosphere inside became dense. So every minute required more attention to load the bus, to make sure the children were sitting down inside, and to leave the stop safe after each pick up.

I reached a stop where a skinny lady asked me, "What's your name?"

"Roman," I replied.

Then I added, "Roman like the Roman Empire."

"OK." She looked at me and then smiled. And she said to me, "Smile, Roman."

Actually, I did smile.

I did not know that my face was tense. I tried to keep a good humor that day. Though inside, I was sad. For sure something was weighing on my stomach. How did she know? I did not have sunglasses on as usual. Maybe she saw through my eyes, since we know our eyes often reflect the expression of our body and mind. Was she a psychologist to notice that something was going on in my life?

The next day, a father, walking back to his car, gave me the two fingers. I proceeded to the next stop; I met the same lady, Angelina, in the stop across from her beautiful mansion. She smiled at me; I smiled back.

By coincidence, I looked down at her feet; I noticed her sandals with a particular sign in them. With my right hand, I told her, "Come in."

She entered the bus. Again, I looked down at her feet. "What does this sign mean?"

With two fingers opened, she said, "This is the sign of peace."

"Wow! They're beautiful."

"Thank you!"

x. Mute Documents

One afternoon of January 2008, I dropped off two students, a boy and a girl, on Dix Highway. The girl was walking in front of the teenage boy, who had his camera phone on and focused it on the girl's butt while she was crossing the street. Sitting on the driver's seat, I was probably the only person in front of the bus to observe this scene. The boy walked straight behind the girl. When she almost finished crossing the street, he moved back in the direction of his home, contemplating the magnificent work just done. I looked at the mirror to check if anybody else on the bus saw what I have seen. Nobody even looked at me. Then I drove away, thinking that I've been a teenage boy too.

xi. Vomit on the Bus

After the morning run, I left Forest Park. I was on the left lane, waiting for the green lights at the intersection of Vanderbilt Parkway and Deer Park Road. Lolita, a school bus driver from my company, asked me, "Do you have a midday?"

"No," I answered. "What's wrong?"

"Somebody vomited on my bus."

"So it's not a big deal."

She raised her eyebrows in a sign of disgust. "I can't drive a bus with that s…"

"Mmm!"

"Can we switch buses, Roman?"

"Nope."

I smiled. The lights turned green, and then we left each other to our own destination.

To be clear, vomit, spit, sh…t are considered normal for me, contrary to some other people. I do not care. In this case, I would just clean it. Isn't it our bus? One day could be our turn to also vomit on it. What's the problem?

Perhaps that driver thought that I have rat's lungs.

xii. Rudimentary Needs

The morning of February 27, 2008, I spent thirty minutes eating breakfast and reading a paper in my favorite spot on Bagatelle Road. The time came to begin to pick up the elementary students. I was about to pull up when another school bus passed me and stopped right in front of me. In order to share a few words with him, I moved my bus and then stopped parallel to his bus. I waited a few seconds. Although he was standing at the door, he could not notice me and never turned. He did not want to turn. He was not finished yet. He could not finish. Nonetheless, the urgencies of that rudimentary need blocked all his other senses and compelled him to stay motionless, because that need was more important than talking to me at that time. He would rather be careful, since he never thought about the possibility of a voyeur who could take advantage of him by recording this scene and publish it on YouTube.

Uuuh! Finally, he could hear the bus engine. He turned his head and raised his eyebrows to share a look of complicity with me. I drove away to begin my run. As a man and a human being, I did not want to disturb his physiological need at that time. Sadly, it is more difficult for a woman to relieve herself when she is in need. I even heard one female driver complaining about some male drivers who have the capacity to do this rudimentary act without the least embarrassment. Here was her commentary one day: "I feel jealous because I cannot do it."

So many times, we feel the urgency to relieve ourselves from this physiological need in places away from a school or from a shopping center. Do not ignore the fact that some male bus drivers carry bottle, cup, gallons, and all kinds of containers. Should that driver be hanged for doing the most rudimentary need where he was not supposed to do it?

I left the case at your attention; as the judge, give the verdict.

xiii. Picky Bus Attendant

I drove a handicapped van for my first year. During a midday, the bus attendant and I had to drive some students to the Veterans Affair Hospital (VA). Among the students who rode the bus, one was really in bad conditions that he began to dribble.

As the driver, my duty required me to push the wheelchair on top of the lift and safely bring the student on the bus. It was not my first time transporting that boy, so I did it without the least embarrassment. Once the student was inside the van, the female bus attendant had to strap all the belts and secure the chair. While I was lifting the student, she looked at me. Her look translated a certain feeling of discomfort. In order to finish quicker, I went inside the bus to help her put the belts. After dropping the students off, she said to me, "Roman, I'm not going to do this route again."

"I don't care doing it every day," I replied.

The dollar always has Washington's picture on it, doesn't it?

xiv. Torture

In June 2009, the first regular week of summer school, I replaced Cecilia, a bus attendant who was running late to work. Carmelo, the wheelchair bus driver, had already left. Because the driveway was narrow, at the stop sign, he had to back up to let the bus attendant's car come into the yard. Since it was her run, Carmelo waved to her and then stopped in order to wait for her. With her right hand, she waved back to Carmelo in a way meaning go ahead. That was what he told me when I asked him, "Why do I have to replace her, since she just came to work?" Then we left.

That day, we left the yard to go to the school. At the school, I understood why she did not want to get on the bus. At the school, to my surprise, Carmelo lifted a handsome boy named Torture. I secured the wheelchair. The boy was shaking; he was spitting. I asked Carmelo, "What his name?"

"Torture," he said. Then he added, "I have been driving him for three years."

"What happened to him? Does he speak?"

"No."

Looking at me through the dome mirror, my eyes met Carmelo's eyes.

With a heavy accent and a melancholic tone, he continued, "When he was a child, his father threw him at a wall. You know, he got brain damage. He stayed in comma for many months. That is why he became disabled."

"Oh Lord, that's cruel!"

Looking at me again, and shifting the van to drive, he was about to leave the school. Then with a tender tone, and a quivering voice, he added, "His father just got out of jail last year. He spent ten years in prison. I only saw his mother once."

Witnessing any human being who has been through this degree of torture, I thought I was dreaming with my eyes wide open.

xv. The Cry of a Dispatcher

A dispatcher represents in some way the axis of the school bus transportation system. He is under constant stress. He faces pressures from the management, from the employees, from mechanics, from the district, and even from students or their parents. People yell at him, he yells back at them or accepts their insults by keeping his mouth shut. His duty does not differ from a commander's. He has to quickly decide in coordination with the driver in case of emergency. He also has to balance schedule; and this is where he can destroy, boycott, or discourage a driver until the latter decides to leave the job. This important task makes some people consider him as their god, if you'd allow me the expression. In consequence, he is in charge of our destiny because he controls our checks. That is why some people pray him, beg him, bend down, or crawl in front of him; others even betray their colleagues in order to receive his favor in return.

Though for all this work, the paradox is, we, school bus drivers, get a better hourly pay than him. This contrast is done purposely in order for him to be extremely rational in his decisions in the repartition of the schedule. Here is the character. One day, I witness one of them crying.

Indeed, a dispatcher from the company, Augustavia, receives pressure from the drivers, the management, the mechanics, pressure from life and its exigencies, etc.

We need to understand the complexity of a dispatcher's job. He has to try to please the management's requirements: Make sure no one gets overtime; watch for a balance of the salaries; the same person cannot make a big check two or three consecutive weeks. And consequently, so many times, he has been harassed by upset employees, whose checks are short or who get paid less than the amount expected.

On many occasions, I have been also underpaid. I personally claim the difference and speak up for what belongs to me. According to the famous Haitian comedian, Fernel Valcourt (Jesifra), "When you're hungry, raise your hand and put it in your mouth, no one else is going to put it for you." In other words, drivers who are shy or too nice and drivers who do not want to complain to dispatch have been cut down so many hours. I even witness a coworker talking to a union member about thousand dollars lost.

As proof, that morning Panamela, a female bus driver, was so furious that she began to talk in a rude manner to Augustavia while using a succession of dirty words that the dispatcher began to feel hot. The heat was so unbearable that she rushed to reach an agreement with Panamela before going to lunch. With a discouraged and unsure pace, her face down in a sign of guilt, misty-eyed, she rushed to her car. Her head in the direction of the unknown, she opened the door, started the engine, then went to lunch.

For sure that afternoon, the lunch had a sour taste in her mouth. How could she digest that food? As an experienced school bus driver, she managed to go and come back safely that day.

It was not a good day. It was not a day like every day, but a day where she just received a slap in her face for being too loyal or too grateful to the employer's exigencies. Much industry and little conscience make us rich(Hervey W. G. Benham). Right! Since the beginning, wealth had been based on, one way or another, a sort of exploitation of others.

That other was a tough one. She hit her so hard with her tongue that she had to think twice if she was endowed with a little conscience. The next time she will have to squeeze somebody's hours, a simple look at the computer screen will reflect her eyes, her face, her conscience, and herself, condemned to serve the employer to the detriment of passive employees. On the screen, she will read her disappointment in life, her problems, her misery, her burden, her pain—the pain she caused herself or at will to so many poor drivers in order to keep a position. Is she happy?

I am sure she is not!

CHAPTER XXI

One Million Eyes Are Watching Us

When driving a school bus, we have the impression that we own that little world, thinking that we are our own master; we are in sole command. Illusion! We are not. And for good, we should never be. Aren't we human beings? We are not free like the seagull, since we are able of doing the worst things when we give ourselves to our deliriums, or when it is a question of satisfying our vile and bestial fantasies. As a matter of fact, a lot—I repeat— a lot of unthinkable things take place inside the school bus, which was supposed to be considered a holy place. In reality, it is not! Indeed, the school officials, the company, the drivers, and the children are aware of this state of fact. As a result of this observation, allow me to say that one million eyes are looking at us. Thus, we are being watched by the police, by the company employees, by the district officials, by other drivers, by parents, and also by the technology.

i. The Police

They say that discipline leads life. As a bus driver, we must respect some principles "and follow the rules of conduct that protect the interests and the safety of all employees and the organization" (EBI Employees Policy

Manual, Feb 2009, p. 31). Among others, we should respect the rules of circulation, follow the traffic signs and patterns of the roads, and ensure the respect and the safety of our passengers.

School bus drivers and police collaborate very well on the roads. As long as we, as school bus drivers, respect the regulations: no speeding, no crazy driving, no cutoffs, etc. Though as human beings, we sometimes make mistakes.

Experience showed me that police often find an evident circumstance to pull us over. They should warn and fine us anytime we act in a way that deviates from the rules of circulation, but not because they want to.

As a matter of fact, zigzagging on the roads, putting this way the safety of the other drivers in jeopardy, is considered a wrong behavior that needs to be disciplined. It is important that the police who usually patrol an area should have an idea of our profile, depending on the frequency of our trips in a particular zone. All the same for us bus driver, people's faces we met very often on the road become familiar to us.

The police's mission calls them to protect us and give us their collaboration when the moment requires it, although some circumstances sometimes force them to use harsh or necessary measures against us.

ii. School Officials

Once in a while, a dispatcher, a safety employee, or the operations manager might call and warn one of us about a dangerous situation. There is any chance somebody has followed the driver in question during the run or during a part of the run. Perhaps, the atmosphere inside the bus was not in accordance with the safety rules. In other words, the children's behavior was not OK, or the driver might let them get off at a street corner or on the other side of a busy street, where a blind spot can cause a fatal accident, and so on.

There are so many regulations that can help us overcome the challenge and the complexity of this job. If any official sees or notices that we do something wrong, they notify the company, which, in turn, warns us.

In November 2007, an accident happened on Bagatelle Road, where one person died. That afternoon, I was going south, and my first stop was before a red flashing light. One boy, who lived on the other side of Bagatelle, usually crossed the street to go to his house. Later after the run, I was called by the safety manager, who ordered me to stop dropping off on this side of the street. Then the company published a paper preventing all drivers from dropping off on the other side of a principal street in the Half Hollow Hills School district.

iii. Employees of the Company

School bus drivers should be aware of the fact that they have been tracked everywhere they go. Because of the human kind's unstable and faithless character, we sometimes need a police officer, a security guard, a commander, or a third eye to watch us. Otherwise, we can go over the limit of our right and abuse it, or act carelessly when performing our duty.

To compensate these inconveniences, unexpectedly, a company employee would follow us during a certain time of the school year. This is part of the safety requirements. School bus drivers, without realizing it, are being tracked by school employees, company officials, parents, or even by other school bus drivers. They can follow us under parents' grievances, under district requirement, or as a simple routine check.

Safety remains the principal motive of this strict routine check. Safety is the first requirement of the transportation system, because we, as school bus drivers, carry precious packages, the future men and women of America. The second motive is the conservation and the renewal of the contracts with the school districts. Therefore, the management, with the aim to do something good and to prevent parents' complaints, will use all kinds of constraints so that the bus drivers perform their duty in full efficiency and appropriately.

The other eyes watching us are the parents.

iv. The Parents

In order to guarantee the safety of their children, in some areas, parents follow us the first school day or almost every day of the first week. Other parents even report a driver's wrongdoing to the school district, or they directly call the phone number of the company posted behind the bus

(Vehicle & Traffic Law of NYS1223a). Multiple reasons can force them to call: dissatisfaction with the order of the route, a poor bus management, unsafe driving, passing red lights, or their own agenda, etc. So many cases to warn us against the dangers of the roads, but are their reports an advantage or disadvantage?

For me sincerely, I have gotten great advantages out of them. Why? Because anytime the company warns me about something, it increases my maturity and expands my field of experience, my responsibility, my sense of duty, my conscience of the environment. It is a sort of equilibrium that makes us better drivers. Instead of annoying us, the parents help and support us; instead of hating us, they love us. Because we are called to perform a job in which the least negligence could lead to disastrous consequences for our life, for the company, for the district, for the parents, for a whole city. We are doing a job that does not tolerate all kinds of mistakes; a job that requires concentration, humility, love of ourselves and love of others; a job that prepares us to smile in a situation to be angry; a job that we are trying to improve using all kinds of important and indispensable tools to help build the students' future.

The next motive is the technology.

v. The Technology

During the last three years, with the continuous desire to technologically modernize the bus company, the top management came up with the GPS. This new tracking device has been installed in almost each school bus. From a computer, a dispatcher or a manager can control our least maneuvers on the roads; they are aware of our speed and our position in real time. So they use it to help or to control certain drivers when necessary. The technology allows a better protection and use of the company's property, especially when they are not aware of some drivers' actions on the roads at a certain time. From a helicopter or on top of a skyscraper, anyone can also see the bus number. The GPS is also a device that would help the police or other authorities to locate and protect the students and us against the probability of an act of kidnapping, or an act of terrorism, or any other incidents on the roads.

Obviously we, as school bus drivers, have no privacy, as no one does in this world. Wherever we are, we have been watched. We do not have any problem being watched by one million eyes because it is an open world; no problem if there is a camera on the bus, in the employees' room, in the yard, or in any other hiding place; if they are doing a study to verify how many times we move our heads during a day or how the children behave on the bus, there is no problem.

Though it was a colleague's problem one Tuesday afternoon April 4, 2010; indeed, I caught that Spanish driver complaining to the operations manager about the cameras. Upset, irritated, his face red, with a violent tone, a high-pitch voice, his hands shaking, he said, "We have cameras watching us everywhere—in the yard, in the employees' room, on the bus, on the trees. Are you going to put a camera in my bedroom also?"

No answer.

My colleague feels that a heavy burden weighs on his shoulder because if he moves, breathes, spits, sleeps, does something wrong, the cameras record it for history. Frankly, that is still no problem.

Our problem is, why not all of us? Why some others in the office, in the safety department are not being recorded? Tell us why! If it is because they are in a better position, it is still not a problem. If not, aren't they employees too? Aren't they also human beings who can commit, like us, all kinds of foolishness? They also need to be disciplined. If we, as school bus drivers, monitors, and attendants, have a silent commander to whip us, a silent witness to watch our slightest move, they need to have one too. They should be watched too as everyone needs to be.

They need cameras to watch their backs because as human beings, they are capable of committing the worst actions. They can abuse their positions; harass other employees; take advantage of people; retaliate against a rude driver; accept backhander; give more hours to relatives, friends, boyfriends, or girlfriends; and the list goes on.

For who does not know or feigns not to know, we are trying our best to tend to accomplish our duty. Perfection and integrity are the only words or qualities that we are trying to cultivate over the years.

The sentiment of selfishness becomes embedded itself deeply in people that they, most of the time, are trying to do things that please themselves instead of others. My cousin Jude explained to me one day that Diogene, the Greek philosopher, held a torch while strolling at noon in the street of Athens. Surprisingly, one of his friends said, "Are you crazy to walk in the sun with a torch?"

Aesop smiled, looked at him straight in the eyes, and then said, "I'm looking for a man."

He was in search of a real, complete, sincere, and perfect man. Can we find one?

Leaders always resist change as much as followers do (John C. Maxwell, *Developing the Leader Within You*, p. 49). If we need real change and transparency for all, it is necessary and even indispensable to have on the roads, on the bus, in the office, or everywhere, for no matter what kind of employee, one million eyes that can replace the eyes of our conscience and keep us away from dangers, troubles, and other incidents.

This refers us to incidents of the roads, the object of the next chapter.

CHAPTER XXII

Incidents And Accidents On The Road

School bus drivers are being exposed to some accidents. Some are direct consequences of our mistakes; others are due to reasons beyond the spectrum of our will. We have experienced some serious and fatal accidents that let indelible scars in our minds. Like our shadow, they will follow us throughout the rest of our life. In light of such considerations, school bus drivers have killed many students. In October 2010, one driver was even killed after an accident with a fuel truck. Let us analyze those accidents successively and unveil their impact on the transportation system.

i. To Begin

"Do you know who had the accident?" I asked a female driver.

She joked, "These bi...s don't know how to drive like you and me."

I responded, "C'mon! It's an accident."

I have to stress out that due to the subtle character of the job, dispatchers and safety employees are wary of giving to other employees any confidential information about another employee. And yet it took me only a few hours to know the details of that accident, for we know that "human's chest is slippery." ("Moun'n gen lestomak glise." A Haitian proverb) In other words, secrets can be held. The French playwright Pierre Corneille said, "Only the graves do not transpire."

When driving a school bus, the least lapse of attention on the job can lead to an incident. Indeed, mistakes always find ways to be filtrated.

ii. Mistake of Inexperience

The Romans said, "To err is human." As a school bus driver, I have made some mistakes due to lack of precaution or lack of concentration.

The first accident occurred one morning in a shopping center located in Huntington. Generally, it is recommended to park the bus in an isolated spot, away from other cars. That way, we diminish the chances of a scratch, a broken mirror, or, in the worst case, to hit another car. That morning, my reflex dictated me that something else could happen. But I did not have the feeling that I was going to break the flashing lights in the back of the bus.

In fact, I was backing up in order to park the bus in a nice and cool spot. I had to control gradually all sides, crossover, rearview mirrors; but I forgot to pay attention to the rear window. The backup alarm was beeping, and the bus was moving smoothly. Suddenly, I heard a noise; I felt that I hit something.

I stopped right away, secured the bus, turned the engine off, took the keys, and got off the bus. I walked to the back to verify the impact. As a result, the back of the bus was bended, and the right flashing lights were shattered. In this case, I violated the employees' work and conduct rules: A negligence or improper conduct leading to damage of employer owned property (EBI Employee Policy Manual, Feb. 09, p. 31). Therefore, I had to assume the consequences.

To tell the truth, in a situation where an accident happened, I, as many other drivers, would rather use my cell phone to call the base than talk in the radio. A cell phone is a more accurate and confidential device. Anytime an accident happens, the dispatcher, the operations manager, the safety manager, and the mechanics need perfect information so they can act quickly and efficiently. In fact, I called the dispatcher and told him about the incident. In less than twenty minutes, the mechanics and safety personal showed up. They took pictures of the bus and the scene. The mechanic chief drove the bus back to the Kings Park Yard, while the safety manager drove me to the doctor for drug test according to the company's policy and according to the 49CFR 382.303 (NYS Laws and Regulations, 2011, p. 61 and 62,) "As soon as practicable following an occurrence involving commercial motor vehicle…each employer shall test for alcohol and controlled substances each surviving driver."

And "a driver who is subject to post-accident testing shall remain readily available for such testing or may be deemed by the employer to have refused to submit to testing."

According to the policy of the company and according to the implied consent, for every incident or accident, as little as it may appear, we, school bus drivers who hold a CDL, have consented to such testing as is required by any state or jurisdiction (49 CFR 383.72, NYS Laws and Regulations, 2011, p. 65). For me, there was no problem in doing a drug test, because I knew that I was going to be cleared.

Sincerely, I felt a little embarrassment for being involved in an accident while I was off duty. I just stopped to buy breakfast. Indeed, the consequences for my mistake were multiple: Lost of my safety and attendance bonus for the month, suspension for three days, and training.

"Life is all about mistake, we should learn from that" (Mark Twain). To be clear, this incident did not have too much repercussion on my mind and body. The next one will have serious consequences.

iii. The Emergency Brake

On Deer Park Road, I had an accident that, even now, I still live and experience the after-effects. That afternoon, I left High School West. With precision and respecting the conditions of safety, I cautiously dropped the students off until I got to the last stop. Generally, it was in my habit to secure the bus by pulling the emergency brake every time I was dropping off; but during that disastrous moment, I forgot and I did not. At a corner across from her house, my last passenger, a girl, got off the bus, then crossed the street. I closed the doors.

I left my seat and began to post-trip the bus. While I was walking to the back, I felt the bus moving. Immediately, I ran back to the front until I reached the emergency brake and pulled it to stop the bus. Too late! The bus went between an electric pole and a basket ball hoop. Consequences: broken glasses in the doors.

As I was in a state of shock, I breathed deeply in order to regain control of my nerve. I took my cell phone and went outside to call base.

In this situation, the safety manager had to call the police, who did a report. As required, she took my license and the DVIR (Driver Vehicle Inspection Report) sheet. Then I had to follow the usual procedures and rules that required me to immediately have a drug test so the company, in case of any investigation, is aware of my blood alcohol content level at this time and also to protect the company against any fictitious lawsuit, as it is usually in this country. Eventually, the tests appeared negative, and I did not get any ticket for the incident.

It is important to underline that there are some bad experiences in life that will traumatize us throughout many years. Some experiences whose repercussions on our body and mind will follow us during a long period of our existence. To tell the truth, until now, I am still experiencing the trauma of this accident. Sometimes, during a post-trip, I still feel the bus moving with me. So I have to hold a seat in order to make sure I am not going to fall.

Once in a while, drivers forget to pull the emergency brake. Thus, allow me to stress that another accident of the same nature is very likely to occur due to the imperfections of the Child Alert System (Different ways to deactivate the button: either we push the silver button in the back with the key in hand or in economic mode, or we open the backdoor) and the short time (fifteen seconds) that requires us to run to the back to post-trip the bus after each trip.

Those scary moments have haunted our spirit and nailed on our mind throughout the night that we sometimes even dream of them.

Obviously, we can understand the Haitian bus driver's traumatism after he had run over a child one afternoon. There is reason enough for him to decide to abandon this job and never drive a school bus again.

iv. Accidents with other Cars

Every day, school bus drivers have been involved in accidents. The table 1 of the Department of Motor Vehicles publishes that 2,414 school vehicles accidents happened in 2009. In particular, I was hit twice by other cars.

a) First Accident

The first accident happened one morning on Carman Road, Dix Hills. I stopped at the entrance of a semicircular driveway to pick up a girl. After two minutes, the mother did not come out. Given that Carman Road is a narrow and busy street, and I did not want to hold the traffic unnecessarily, after a few seconds, I stepped on the accelerator to leave. Immediately, the mother opened the door to bring the child. I stopped on the other end of the driveway. I felt a slight jolt that shook the bus. I looked at the left mirror. A van was behind the bus. It crashed on the back bumper. I turned off the engine, secured the bus, and took the keys. I walked to the back of the bus to verify if any damage, scratch, bend, leak, etc., was visible. The hood of the van was bended. The driver came in the front to assess the damages. For the record, I wrote on a piece of paper all the necessary and important information from the van: license plate number, make, color, etc.

I approached him and said, "Are you OK?"

He despised me first and later began to protest that it was my fault. I did not reply because, as a bus driver's rule, "Do not discuss the accident with anyone. Answer only question the police ask about the accident. Talk only to representative of the Company" (EBI Policy Manual, Collisions/Incidents Procedures for all Vehicles, p. 41, sec. 9).

The student's mother came to my assistance; she argued with him, saying, "As a witness, she will explain the situation to the police."

You can deduct the police decision in this case. One more time, I had to spend at least three hours to complete the procedures and the regulations anytime an accident happens.

That accident was a minor one compared to the next one.

b) Second Accident

The other accident happened in summer 2007. I just dropped off some students from a summer day camp to the movie theater located in the Broadway Mall, Hicksville. Coming out of the mall, I kept the right lane. That morning, it was drizzling. The traffic lights just turned green. A few seconds after, I moved the bus that was about to turn left on Route 106 when I heard a screech of tire. I looked at the direction of the noise: a truck skidded and headed straight toward my bus. The driver was struggling to stop. I floored the pedal to accelerate and prevent the crash. Too late! The roads were slippery. The truck run the red lights, hit the car, which, in its turn, hit and damaged the engine door and bent the left side bumper.

No injuries were reported. The car's driver got out safe and sound of his car.

Four or five seconds after, the truck passed the red lights. A significant time! What was he thinking about? He and he alone knew. Perhaps he had too many bills or too much family problems; perhaps for being too tired, he was sleeping behind the steering wheel. So many questions that only he and his conscience can answer.

To my female coworker, the least inattention while driving can lead to a disaster. Apart from the different definitions of accident (17NYCRR 722.1, NYS Laws and Regulations, 2011, p. 9), accident means, according to the Macmillan Dictionary, "an unfortunate event that is not expected or intended." Like you suggested, it is not a question of you and I are the best bus drivers. The question is that they are like us real people, capable of making mistakes and also sometimes capable of preventing other drivers' wrongdoing.

Other or all things being equal, accident should happen without apparent cause or reason. Accident is something that we cannot prevent, something that we did not have any nose or the least hint about, something that can happen but we should not be the cause. At times, accidents can be premeditated. Regardless of the reasons, we should try to avoid accidents anytime we find a minimum chance. Material or vengeful reasons, neglect, hope of a lawsuit, etc., do not justify any accident. Accidents should be spared because we do not know what the ultimate consequences could be. Oftentimes, the consequences could be injury, lost of lives, desperation of an entire family's future, and even our own death.

c) Tribute to a Colleague

It was a foggy and damp day of autumn; the morning star, feeling the arrival of a sad event, suddenly lost its splendor and stopped glittering. And the sun was shy to raise and illuminate the town of Copiague, for it was going to set the stage for a sad and unprevented event—my friend Jasmin Clériné died in an accident. Indeed, his flat nose bus was crushed after hitting a tanker. And consequently, that Haitian school bus driver, with a contagious smile, that coworker I met for the first time at West Hollow Middle School in Melville, died three days after atrocious pains and sufferings.

We are not allowed to judge what has happened that morning or to draw a conclusion from the vain commentaries people have made about the disaster. We also hope that people will not be angry at us if we dare say something relating to such a tragedy. In reality, we do not know the circumstances or the causes of the accident; we do not know if it was a mechanical failure, dizziness, distractions, etc. Yet they say that the school bus is the safest vehicle. Did he forget that he was driving a flat nose bus that does not give him any protection? Or did he pretend to have the right of way, and because of that, he was just driving blindly to his direction as many other drivers do when they are sure they will have a no-fault accident? Perhaps, he did not like his transfer from one school district to another for insufficient reasons; perhaps, he was upset with the state of the things in the company; perhaps, he had family problems; perhaps, he died from his wounds due to his faithful conviction. We do not question that. One thing is sure, now he is not.

And such as we are for now, we cannot predict what will happen to us tomorrow. Therefore it is also important for all of us to step back and think twice as school bus drivers. Man made the bus, and everything we, imperfect human beings, invent or produce has its imperfections and its limits. Thus, it is a fact that perfection goes beyond the spectrum of our understanding. In light of such considerations, the way he died brought to the surface the possibility that it could be another one of us, or one day, it could be us.

Jackto, another one of us, who used to work in the same yard with Jasmin in Copiague, told me that they always had problems with Jasmin because he always began his route earlier. He liked to be on time; and fearing of rushing in the roads, he adopted this precept in the fable, "Slow but steady wins the race" (The Hare and the Tortoise, Aesop).

I pertinently knew Jasmin, an open and easygoing friend, always smiling; he always found a joke to make me laugh. He was also known for his traditional breakfast in the West Hollow Middle School cafeteria: Haitian bread and avocado. And to remind some of my colleagues who could not remember him, I brought this menu to their attention. Jasmin was also a man of great heart, who used the least opportunity to bring a relative here in America. He told me that he had helped more than sixteen family members to move to the USA. As a father, Jasmin cultivated the sense of sacrifice any real father should manifest in working hard to bring the daily bread on the table, to love his family with all his body and his heart, and to worship God. Obviously, as a human being, Jasmin liked his life; he liked the world and enjoyed some of its pleasures. Jasmin loved people; people loved Jasmin.

For forty minutes, the fear of being abandoned, the fear to leave invaded him and probably made him cry. A cry of regret for not having time to accomplish whatever he wanted to, a cry of remorse for saying goodbye this way. Three days of agony. He was strong in front of death. "Death is a too serious thing to face it in a hebetude state" (La mort est chose trop sérieuse pour l'affronter en état d'hébétude. The death of Socrates, Plato). While in pieces and bloody, and to show the police who came to rescue him that he was OK, he gave them the thumbs up!

We share with him our deep sympathies that are nothing compared to the extent of his pains. Are we so extreme to dare believe that he was not happy to wish such a hideous end? Since that day, Jasmin is neither American, nor Haitian, nor Caribbean, nor West Indian, but a citizen of the world, a cosmopolitan.

And yet his family and close relatives will experience a feeling of total desolation, deep sorrow, complete despair, and extreme emptiness; and it will take them time to get rid of it. Jasmin, my friend, as the Haitian saying goes, "Do your time, quit the time. We did not come to stay. It is the law of life. You first, we after; one day we will meet (Isnar Doubi, System Band: Hommage a Ti Mitou, 2007).

Jasmin will live for memorials years in the heart of whoever he has met.

Alfred de Musset said in Tristesse, "God is talking, we must answer him." Therefore, we must answer something inside that does not die, because "God makes us capable of finding happiness even in the death." And like the others, "Jasmin showed up, after, he must disappear" (Sermon sur la mort, Jacques B. Bossuet). Sadly, fifty-six years just disappeared in one morning. Later, his body will disintegrate "to become a 'I don't know what' that doesn't have a name in any language" (Florens Tertullien).

Rest in peace, brother!

v. Children Left on the Bus

After dropping off the last student, drivers must post-trip their bus. Even after post-tripping my bus, a kind of skeptical doubt invades me when doing it the last time in the yard. Many unfortunate drivers have faced this scary and uncomfortable situation where they found students sleeping on the bus.

According to the 8NYCRR 156.3e4 (NYS Laws and Regulations, 2011 p.94), "Drivers, monitors and attendants shall check their vehicle to ensure that no child is left behind on board unattended at the conclusion of the school bus route." And the Section 22 of the Employee Policy Manual states, "It is the drivers, monitors and attendants' responsibilities to be sure that all passengers have left the bus at the last drop off for each route segment. All areas of the vehicle should be checked for sleeping passengers. Failure to follow this policy will be subject to disciplinary action up to and including dismissal." As a matter of fact, we as school bus drivers from EBI must, after checking our bus, call the base and say, "Bus number x cleared, no sleeping children," and make sure a dispatch answers us, "10-4."

During the last two years, the company has enforced this measure. Indeed, at the completion of each school run, and anytime, parking and turning off the ignition, all school bus drivers from the Kings Park Yard should look under the seats in search of any hidden child; they should also push the button alarm (No child left behind device), and lift the emergency backdoor handle (Educational Bus Company Times, April 16, 2010, p. 2,).

As a precautionary measure, if I have the slightest doubt about a post-trip, on my way back to the base, I pull over a second time to make sure that I have completely checked the bus for sleeping children. Now in our company, it's becoming a must to check the bus after each trip, given that the Child Synovial System's alarm will go off automatically.

CHAPTER XXIII

Purpose Of The Child Synovial System Or Child Safety System Or Child Alert System

To face the laxness of certain drivers who do not post-trip their buses and with the aim of improving its service to the community, the company has installed the Synovial Child Check System or the Child Synovial System or Child Safety System or Child Alert System. Its purpose is "to prevent passenger from being left on the company's vehicle." In essence, the Child Synovial System means also no child left behind on the bus. In other words, the bus should be cleared of any passenger after each run. And yet make no mistake about it. Until now, drivers are still leaving children on the bus.

Thus, whoever makes such a mistake will be fired! In fact, to overcome those inconveniences, the company has adopted various measures. The Child Synovial System is the latest. At the beginning this system, like all systems, it has had some imperfections that needed to be corrected. It was blamed for not being a homogeneous system. In brief, we should have one and only one way to deactivate the button for all buses. Not different ways as it is now. For example, for some buses, we have to turn the switch in economic mode, then run to the back to press the button; for others, we have to open the back emergency door; for other buses, we have to take the key off the ignition and go push the button, etc. Different ways that disturb the bus driver who, one day, can find himself in a situation to rush to push the button (in fifteen seconds, the alarm will go off) and can forget to secure the bus, as was the case for one friend and coworker at the beginning of September 2009.

Although the main purpose of the Child Synovial System is to prevent school bus drivers, bus attendants, or driver's assistants from leaving children on the bus, most of the time, our instinct guides us to search for the button instead of searching for children left on the bus. Therefore, for the goods of the cause, we should instinctively assign a dual purpose to our post-trip: look for children and push the button.

In spite of its nonhomogeneous character and the insignificant portion of time allowed to post-trip the bus, the Child Synovial System is an important tool that assumes its purpose in reminding lax school bus drivers to post-trip their buses so that no child will be left behind in this dangerous and rotten world.

CHAPTER XXIV

Observation Of A Sudden Change Of Work Conditions

EBI is one of the best and ideal transportation companies to work in. The staff 's rational management of this company, the fair treatment of its employees, its discipline, its rigor when it comes to question of principle, its knowledge of the environment, and the atmosphere of family that exists make it one of the enviable places where someone might choose to build a career. That is why people who enter have less chance to leave. Although during the last three years, some managers have adopted some extreme measures that do not please the majority of the drivers. In fact, a wind was blowing, and its immediate effect was to change the company from its normal flowing. And as circumstances dictate, many drivers who never hide their resentment had to speak up. Let's develop in details the different subtleties accompanying the job of school bus driver.

i. Benefits of the Job

The company provides a variety of benefits plans (EBI policy Manual, Feb 09, p.16), each one with its advantages and disadvantages. After our probation period, we have the choice between Package 1 and Package 2. Our status will depend on our choice.

Package 1 offers holiday pay, snow days, bereavement leave, bonuses, 401K, profit sharing, life insurance, health insurance, dental insurance, and EAP (Employee Assistance Program). When I first came to the company, I chose Package 1; the next year, I switched to Package 2.

If we choose Package 2, we get two dollars more per hour, no snow days, no insurance. We are also responsible for 100 percent of the health premiums should we decide to participate (EBI Policy Manual, p. 24). We also obtain a flat fifty-dollar bonus every month.

ii. Hour and Salary

At the beginning of the school year, bus drivers sign on average thirty-hour contract with the company. During the last three years, the new managers have been entrusted with the mission to squeeze the hours and let little room for maneuver to drivers. There is nothing wrong in a rigorous management, whose primary mission is to maximize the profit of the company. We also should be in a position to understand that the managers' decisions are consequences of direct pressure from higher instances. Therefore, any ideal manager's mission would be to fairly, rationally, and rigorously apply the principles for each driver.

Consequently, many senior drivers, who do not have a chance to get a midday during the pick run, sometimes have to pressure the managers into giving them one to complete their schedule. In particular, as a senior driver, I need better hours; and in some circumstances, when I notice a kind of bias in the repartition of hours, I weigh my words and claim with tact and respect what belongs to me. If I meet the least opposition from the management, I use facts (safety, seniority, attendance) to convince them. If I feel that they ignore my request, I keep asking until I find an answer.

Indeed, for that particular reason in 2008, I had a virulent argument with a manager about my hours. Not too long ago, during summer 2010, I was upset in a point that I had to speak up to explain and convince a manager about a charter that underpays. For now, management gives another meaning or another description to every route we used to do before as supplementary work (supplementary work means hours that are not included in our regular schedule or more hours than what we have signed for). Therefore, almost everything we do now is a charter. According to the manager, "The Company cannot allow us to do one-hour overtime."

We do not ask for overtime, but for a fair diversification of the salaries and a guarantee, that way, of a proportional and logical distribution of work to all employees. That is what makes sense.

In a certain sense, do all drivers have the same exigencies? Not really. Indeed, some drivers do not care about mistakes in their checks while others are always asking for a regularization of their salary. Mistakes happen so often that if we keep claiming our money some people look at us as if we are the problem instead of being someone looking for solutions to his problems.

In reality, our complaints are based on different grounds.

iii. Complaints Based on Different Grounds

Now, we might ask ourselves these questions, "Why is it like that? Why cannot we, all drivers from the same company, unify ourselves and talk the talk with one voice?"

It is because we are not on the same wavelength. As a matter of fact, let us make it clear, in the school bus transportation system are working a lot of retired and housewife drivers who probably already have either a pension or a social security check or a small business or other benefits. And I have seen drivers who protest against the fact they give them too many hours. Since they have other ways to compensate their expenses, the weekly check is not completely indispensable for their subsistence. While for us old, non-retired, young, or middle-age drivers—single or married—our weekly check is our means of subsistence. Our life depends on it. Therefore, even if some might apparently empathize with us regarding some legitimate complaints, in reality, our complaints do not have the same grounds. That is one reason why there is no true solidarity between the employees. That lack of solidarity makes us sometimes feel like being caught into a trap. We need to have courage and be strong in order to get out.

Depending on our strength of character or our position face to that situation, we could be seen as a traitor or a coward. The more docile we are, the more favor we will get. Thus, if we choose to live a docile life, we will only live a life of favor. Ipso facto, "we continue to live without reason to live," as the music said. Should we stop fighting for what belongs to us? Therefore, we stop breathing; we stop being a human.

Living is a choice. Consequently, this rigorous management and other legitimate reasons force some experimented senior drivers, who do not want to live that way and, in search of a better treatment, to act decisively. In view of this reality, many of them who do not have the courage to fight for their rights just leave the company against their will and go to work somewhere else. They just disappear and leave those managers. As John C. Maxwell puts it, "People join company and leave managers."

iv. Different Impacts on Our Bonus

The fragile context of this job makes it difficult for the management to require constancy from fickle employees. In view of the fact that it is not easy to find drivers who want to drive a school bus and do a career in the industry, and because some drivers of the aforementioned category do not work regularly, we school bus drivers who consider this job as our job, suffer from their laxness. For that complex situation and for economical reasons, the bonus can have different impacts on our checks. Is it a right, the law, or a favor? Its method of calculation penalizes lax or negligent drivers whose comportment deserves to be blamed. In other words, it affects drivers who do not work regularly, the ones who miss work very often, or the ones who have an accident of any kind. We miss one day this week, we feel the pain on the next check and on the bonus of the month; if our car breaks down, we lose our bonus; we have an accident, we lose our bonus; we are sick, we lose our bonus.

Do not forget that we, as migrants, are not supposed to be sick. That is our motto. Our name is Cecilia, that female character in one famous Haitian music talking about the life of a migrant in the diaspora. Cecilia symbolizes the sense of discipline of the migrants working in the factories. Cecilia never laments; she never stops fighting and never abandons the job. Cecilia moans every morning when the clock rings;

her body hurts and she has back pain, but she has to go because she must go to work. If not at her own risks!

Our question is, "Do these sanctions stop drivers from being lax? Or does cutting up our bonuses solve those problems?

v. The Lost of Bonus

In our life, we have learned some lessons that we will never forget. To prove this, here is what happened to me one morning. After doing the pretrip inspection, on my way out, anytime the front wheel hit a bump, the steering wheel moved under my hands, a strange reaction that gave me the feeling that something wrong was happening. As a new driver, I thought it was the steering wheel; but on the contrary, it was the consequence of an overused font tire.

At Candlewood Middle School, after breakfast, I inspected the bus that morning. I noticed a front tire without any threads to grip the road. For sure, I had the responsibility to report this safety defect in order to get that tire changed. And yet due to reasons beyond my control, I forgot to report it that day.

The next day, on my way back after the morning route, the safety manager called me and all the drivers who had driven that bus during the previous week. We all have lost the bonus for the month. It was a necessary and important warning to all of us, bus drivers, who have failed to fulfill our duty with all the cares and the precautions that it requires.

vi. A Surprising Bonus

It was a Friday morning, a senior driver, after switching from Package 1 to Package 2, received the shock of her life. In fact, she almost fell of emotion one day of mid-December when she got her bonus. That lady opened the envelope. I saw her open her mouth and hold her chest with the right hand. She looked at me; I stared back at her. Disappointment was visible in her face. Her eyes have lost their brightness.

Something wrong happened. I said, "Are you OK?"

She said to me, "Roman, I almost have a heart attack."

"I see that. Why?" I replied.

"Look. I just switched to Package 2."

I looked at the check: one-hundred-some change in dollars.

She continued with a shaking voice, "I had more than one thousand dollars the last time before I switched to Package 2."

"Aren't you aware of the risks? You're caught at your own game."

"That's not fair!"

vii. An Unfair System: A Strange Disparity

Today, I am exposing an unfair system that needs to be changed. A sort of disparity exists between school bus drivers and the other employees in the same company. You would say the leitmotiv of this disparity is paradoxically to keep us away from varying degrees of evolution as workers. We are like the broken link of the organization chart. As a link of the chain, we feel isolated, neglected by some irrational and illogic laws that exist. Even some of ours in the crowd of drivers, who after being transferred to other positions, adopt some discriminatory attitudes to satisfy their direct managers' will or to secure their positions. Indeed, they improvise while doing their first managerial test on us by applying some harsh measures. Sadly, they are writing the word attitude with the wrong hand. We somehow feel that we, school bus drivers, are the donkey in the Aesop's fables. Indeed, to repeat Isaac Bashevis Singer, "We are direct victims of man, an animal whose ideals, motivations, and rationalizations are nothing but a wolfish dialectic."

As school bus drivers who are driving students, we have nothing compared to the other employees of the same company: no sick days, no vacation, nothing. We are not supposed to be sick. Is it a tacit consensus? Dear reader, do you ever think one day about the state of mind of the one driving your child?

In fact, during a refresher in Hicksville, my question to a safety employee was, "Don't you think it is necessary for school bus drivers to visit a psychologist every year so that the company can have an idea of its drivers' state of mind?" A lady of a certain age, sitting in the middle of the room, turned back and gave me the thumbs up. Ironically, the employee did not answer my question. Probably he did not understand me, or it was of little importance, or he did not want to raise such a question to a higher instance. The question is still outstanding to the concerned authorities. "Isn't it necessary for us, school bus drivers, to visit a psychologist every year?"

The system should at least give us something. Even if we are the thumb, we still belong to the hand. It is unfair to take everything from us.

viii. Firing of Employees

Since I have been driving in this company, I have witnessed many employees leaving the job. Some leave for justifiable reasons or by their own will, others in search of better treatment or after a conflict with a manager or with a parent, etc. Sometimes they just disappear, and later, we get the news of all kinds of speculations about their dismissals. For reasons of principle, I am not going into the details of those dismissals. But it is real and palpable that every day on the job, our days are being counted while doing this easy job.

ix. School Bus Driver: An Easy Job

Dear school bus drivers, aren't there some days that we feel our hearts beating faster than normal? Many people and many school bus drivers might disagree with me. Though as easy as this job may appear, for people who are not drivers, let me state this for you, "All school bus drivers have a sword of Damocles hanged on top of their heads." Make no mistake about it! The least inattention can lead to some disastrous incidents that can affect our life and, consequently, our family's life. Truly, many drivers were demonized, fired, or even sentenced for some legitimate reasons and, also, for some bogus ones. I agree that discipline leads the world. But it cannot only go one way. As long as it is that way, there will be conflicts, hatred, frustrations, or disasters—consequences of our madness and our irrational decisions when managing.

x. Irrational Decisions

Sometimes the decisions of the managers are irrational and based on simple will. As human beings leading other human beings, they should not abuse their power when they have to make some key decisions.

An improper order can cause conflicts, raise arguments, or even justify employees' complaints. As proof, on January 17, 2011, I was talking to a friend before a dispatcher interrupted me and rudely ordered me to park the buses properly in the backyard. His immoderate tone of voice translated a curse. Stunned, my friend asked me, "Roman, you've problem with him?"

"Don't worry! I'm older than him," I replied.

Probably somebody just yelled at him; thus, he did nothing but transmit the shock on me. Why didn't he buy a whip? His order reminds me of my brother-in-law's commentary about his manager, "This guy curses me in a way that gives me the feeling he'll flog me one day."

Being the case, there were days when our frustrations reached the highest level. With time, we age in the night of time and learn to approach the world scrupulously, with kindness, with parsimony and an open and conciliatory desire.

Moreover, I always keep in mind the famous Haitian comedian Languichatte Debordus's lesson (Theodore Beaubrun, La Vi New York), which stipulates, "America is a school, a school where we learn to face the hard reality of life." I agree. Please allow me to add, "America is more than a school. It is also a nursery, where depending on our childish behavior, the reality will correct us as a child; America, a college, whose degree prepares us to learn to live in the true sense of the term: cautiously approach life with all the good in it; America, a university, where we master suffering for the rest of our lives if we have been living a delirious life throughout our teenage years; America, a film, where each scene hides a deep truth that opens our book and unveils our nudity; America, a fable that alludes to us and teaches us wisdom and morale lessons that are valid today and will remain *ad vitam aeternam*; America, a…Let me stop here!"

We know how shocking my observation might be to a category of good people. If I am lying, please may one driver have the courage to refute me. After all, my purpose is not to please or displease anyone. I have lived, I am still living, and I have observed people complaining about this sinister situation. These are real facts. I take the courage to speak no matter what the issue will be. With the serenity of an experienced observer, I have pursued research and questioned other drivers. Indeed, my purpose is to reveal what is worth revealing. Albert Einstein has proved and demonstrated that all is relative. Those who are on the same train with me can see the trees moving, while the others, who are out, see the train moving instead. It is of great importance for me to draw this observation for the others. It is the fall of a stone on a hill that has hit many obstacles and finally stops on my heart; the shock hurts; there is nothing I can do but cry to react.

The fact is that in a company, any time production prevails over human factor, or profit over employees' well-beings, or any time extreme and rational management system gains right over ideal conditions of work for a category, that category will rise and claim, even in the face of death, its rights. The world history has already proven that.

In consequence, we feel a sort of empty space that needs to be filled in. We can hear from the distance a clock ringing, an imminent reverse needs to take place. As the Haitian poet Etzer Vilaire wrote in his book *Les Dix Hommes Noirs*, "A clock rang, a man is coming. The clock rings already, but when is coming the man?" (Une heure a sonne, un homme doit venir. L'heure sonne déjà, mais quand donc viendra l'homme?)

Voilà, somewhat many reasons, many biased and distorted rules that go one way, many sad consequences, many legitimate and justifiable requests, many arbitrary, improvised, and irrational decisions that translated a sudden change of work conditions and automatically gave birth in the employees' mind the idea of the presence of a union in order to regulate the situation in the company and bring a sort of equilibrium in the balance so that everyone, not some drivers, can find a little place under the sun and enjoy the comfort of a warm life.

That leads us to the birth of the union.

CHAPTER XXV

The Birth Of The Union

Basically, human beings' worst conditions awaken in them some normal reactions and some legitimate sentiments. As proof, we could feel a wind of change that was blowing in people's faces and winkled them with belief that only by the presence of a union could the reign of arbitrary and improvised management be stopped.

i. The Invasion

It was 6:00 a.m., I went to the back to get a bus to cover a route. Surprisingly, in all corners of the yard, I saw people handing tracts to the employees. Some drivers accepted them; others refused, while some others waited until they were out of the field of vision of the cameras to get one. Indeed, an invasion took place. It reminded me of the US Army's invasion of Haiti to get rid of the military government in 1994. With the only difference, the army had M-16, tanks, and other death's tools to destroy anyone who dared face them since they needed to create space, while the union handed papers using words that can change people's hearts. Doesn't the Word say, "In the beginning was the Word" (John 1:1)?

According to a friend's statement, after I left the yard, "Some employees in the management, where *things are doing well*, went to chase away the invaders who did not want to leave the yard." One of the invaders warned them, "Get out of here! This isn't your land." This retort translates an indirect way to remind this category of employees that they have no rights to accuse them of trespassing or no legal capacity to file any lawsuit against them.

Indeed, the man, the union has come. He has come too late in a world too old (Alfred de Musset, La Confession d'un Enfant du Siècle). What can he do? Can he protect and support our cause? Does his presence means hope? Is he a man of salvation who will lead us to achieve our goal, which is a better treatment in the application of the rules? Does his presence means no cut of hours? Can the ambiance of family that existed before come back? Does he have the magic to make this lover of marble move? In brief, can the union fulfill its mission, which calls it to pave the way for one category of employees, the school bus drivers, to fairly coexist with the other employees in an ideal world?

ii. The Election

Before the election took place, let me clarify a point. The urgent demands of the moment and the fear of losing their jobs put pressure on the instigators of the movement. In fact, they had to carefully handle the goat and the cabbage. One of them even dared offer me the possibility of becoming the coordinator of the movement. As an individual, in my life's story, I never blindly embrace any cause. I like to observe and be aware of its aim before coming part of it.

When it was time to elect a representative, many candidates who stood for a post withdrew their candidacy either at will or dissatisfaction with the process, or because the ones who called the union stayed away just to save their skins, or perhaps for fear of retribution.

Two people were elected. One of them resigned later because he found another job. The only representative left to fight for us is still there.

iii. Give and Take Rule: The Contract

In life, people should learn to give in order to receive.

The union came; a new contract has been established. Due to human being's insatiable character, when it was time to vote, some bus drivers who wanted more than what was in the contract had their backs to the wall. Clearly, we have been under pressure during that period. A kind of mobilization took place in order to force the employees to vote yes. An employees' representative, who was trying to turn my intention of voting, said to me, "If this contract doesn't pass, I will resign." After a discussion with a representative of the union about the content of the contract, his warning to me was, "If you guys don't vote yes, the company will kick us out." And yet, although everyone I know voted no, because the majority was not satisfied with the clauses of the contract, the result was yes.

Being now an agreement between the company and the drivers, what does the contract give? What have we gained from it? Will the birth of the union bring real change that will satisfy our legitimate and reasonable request for a search of happiness?

CHAPTER XXVI

In Search Of Happiness

A winter morning, on my way down Pulaski Road, I passed the same jogger, his head straight looking forward and his strong legs defying the icy braise. When I reached the yard, the barometer indicated 14 degrees F. I got off my car, and I began to cough from the contact of the cold wind. I zipped on my jacket to the collar in order to protect my chest from the cold breeze, and I rushed to my bus. When I stepped inside the bus, I looked at the dashboard; and I turned on all the heaters, the defrosters, and the lights. As required, I began to do the pretrip inspection.

I walked to the back of the bus. While outside, I slowly turned my head 130 degrees to observe all the buses around me. They have been turned on so their engines warmed up before any driver began to drive them. I turned my head to contemplate all the buses, to contemplate the power of money, the power of the American system, the power of discipline. After the pretrip inspection, as usual, I moved forward and parked my bus near the dumpster. I opened the door of the employees' room and greeted the people inside. As usual, some answered me; some did not. From the coffeemaker pot, I poured some fresh coffee in a cup; and from the water cooler, I cooled it down with some cold water. Indeed, I had to drink it fast.

While I was standing and contemplating the paintings inside the employees' room, a driver with heavy Spanish accent told me, "A few more days."

Charly, another American driver, responded, "Yes, babe, a whole week off."

"This is not fair. A whole week without pay."

"You collect unemployment benefit."

"Yeah! But you'll get half the money."

"Let me tell you. This is not a job for someone with two kids. This is not a job for someone with a normal family."

This phrase went straight to my heart. For a moment, I felt petrified, as if these words nailed me down on the ground. I took a sip of coffee, and with great pain, I swallowed it. Given that I knew I had four daughters and a lot of people to help, I didn't say a word. Wait a minute! I checked the time in my cell phone. It was time to leave.

I entered the bathroom to get some paper towel. On my way out of the door, a driver was about to enter. He said to me, "Is it safe?"

To tease him, I replied, "Haitian spices in action. Not a good time, bro!"

I returned to my bus to begin the route. I began to drive that day, wondering what my next job will be. In my life, I have never dreamed to be a school bus driver. But now it's real and evident: I'm driving a school bus every day. Should I accept this reality and continue on as a school bus driver until the end of my days? Or should I stop complaining, ignoring the bad sides of the job, and begin to approach it with a positive attitude? As a matter of fact, I embrace Uncle Jacob's advice to little Albert Einstein who was questioning his job of being a shoemaker. "My boy, try to do work you love. And if you find yourself in a spot where you have to do work that you dislike, you must find a way of making yourself like it so that you can do it well" (Albert Einstein, Arthur Beckhard, p. 16). Another way to say no matter what job we do or we have done, no matter what task we perform, we always get paid with the dollar bill; we always see Washington's picture on the paper. Is there a place in the dollar where the job "bus driver" or any other job is written?

We should fight here and get rid of all kinds of our complex; we should try to improve our skills, and, consequently, increase our ability, our chance to succeed in America.

Being a migrant living in America, I have been forgotten, exploited, neglected by some others, or even paradoxically by people from my own country. I have to fight every day to survive. The world appears sometimes mean, for there are friends or relatives that I will never see again; there are others who will feel discouraged, abandoned, ignored, disabled; others will become old, weak, or sick under the weight of the ages. Many will disappear; others will die.

I have found out of a dear family member's death years after, and the sad news still weights on my stomach for not being able to tell her at least one comforting word before she passed away. So many others had disappeared in the catastrophic earthquake of January 12, 2010. I left Haiti to come to live in America in search of something better; I came here with a noble, bold, and sublime goal in mind; I came to respond to some difficult and challenging questions that need scrupulous and careful answers. I am the owner of my own destiny. I will achieve my goal or create this ideal only if I seek that destiny.

Fate is not going to shape my future. Hard work, self-discipline, the sense of sacrifice, a positive mind, and many other qualities can help me achieve or build it. Success is not an end in itself; it is a process that requires years of preparations and conceptions.

That strong and redoubtable jogger, that I pass every morning, has every chance to win the competition for sacrificing his time, energy, and many other activities in order to prepare his body and mind. Like him, I am looking at the trophy of happiness over there at the horizon. Should I reach it? I do not know. The only sure thing I know is that I'm running toward it.

CHAPTER XXVII

Antwann Joseph

My friend's first son was living in the Bronx. He was around four years old when his mother moved to the USA. During a conversation with his reunited father, he begged him to gain custody of him. Indeed, he explained to him clearly. "Dad I'm twelve now. I've nobody to watch me, to protect me against the aggressions of the students in my school. My mother never attended a school's meeting with a teacher."

He sadly confessed to the father that he was forced to follow, the laws and the rules of the streets. In case he refused, they would have punished him. Antwann Joseph's story is similar to that boy's.

Antwann does not know his father. Son of a Haitian-American, he is among thousands of other American children abandoned by their fathers either by bad will or for fear of being victim of the system. Antwann's last name is Joseph because it is said that, years ago in Haiti, the registry officer just chose deliberately the name Joseph for any child who did not have a father.

Antwann belongs to the category of children whose single mothers never attend a meeting in the school, because they cannot either afford missing a workday, which would have serious consequences on their paychecks, or they just gives up indifferently.

On different occasions, I had the honor to drive Antwann to school. Let me present to you this wonderful boy.

i. The Bus Stop

Antwann waits alone for the bus on the curbside. The cold air sweeps his immaculate face. The rigor of winter, the rain, the snow, the chilly wind never forces him to resign.

Antwann never complains; he never feels discouraged even if he has to wait longer for the bus. He never goes back home to sleep; he never murmurs a word to draw our attention. Some days, this strong little boy waits across from his friend's house, a few feet away from his stop.

Antwann is a soldier, a bold cavalier, a particular hero, a fighter ready to follow the command, ready to fight, in front of the battalion, a fight which doesn't leave blood, deaths, or moans. Its goal is not greed, or thirst of power. This is another fight. Antwann fights in search of one noble goal, one conviction, one ideal in mind, or "a dream to create the future" (Victor Hugo). In fact, he goes to school in search of the bread of instruction, a path to the well-being.

In the morning, before boarding the bus, Antwann plays football with his friends who live across the street. When it is too cold in the morning, the other boys stay inside. Everyone, except him, is inside. He stands across from their house. The other children are looking at him through the door; he is looking back at them. Probably he has something to say; no one wants to hear him.

Today I think his friend's mother would hear his silent supplications and would invite him to come and enjoy the heat of the house for a few minutes before the bus comes. She might be scared to invite him to enter when we know the multiple interpretations that that invitation might lead to. Even though some people, who are endowed with a surge of fraternity, take a risk in the sense of good in spite of the consequences their act can cause.

The same way, I risked the consequences the second week of the run when the boy's mother came at the corner stop to ask me if I could pick up the children in front of her house because she was nursing a baby. At first, I refused by telling her to follow the regular process. "Ma'am, I have no problem picking them up in front of your house. Just call the school district to ask them to change the stop." Later, I understood her as a mother; she didn't want her newborn to face that rigorous winter. The next day, I decided by myself, at my own risks, to pick up the students in front of her house.

Madame, please let this boy come inside the same way this white woman, one winter morning, offered me to come in the warm comfort of her office to wait for the transit bus on Route 112. I still remember that morning. Probably that woman forgets her act of charity. Indeed, I was working an overnight shift as a security guard in a warehouse located in Coram. When it was 5:00 a.m., another guard, a retired man who came to replace me said, "Where do you live?"

"Huntington," I replied.

Then he added, "Where's your car?"

"I don't have a car. I take the bus home."

"What a shame!"

That cold morning, I left the building. On Route 112, that woman saw me soaking in the frigid air at a bus stop. The cold rays of the sun illuminated my whole body, and I frowned when the light breeze whipped the little uncovered portion of my face. Any reasonable human observing me can imagine how cold I was. It was around 8:00 a.m. That woman had compassion for me. You know, woman! She was surely a mother. She understood how hard it was for me, a tropical man, to remain petrified in the cold, waiting for the bus. Did I remember her name or her face? I'm not sure. What was important was the act, this surge of fraternity, her pity for me. I will never forget her!

Like this white woman, probably a mother, who has helped me, an unknown man in the street, an unknown black man whose heart and intentions she did not know, Madame, please the next time, do the same for the next Antwann, a harmless child in your neighborhood who will need to fight the onslaught of a rigorous winter.

ii. Victim of Influence

Antwann Joseph belongs to this category of students who become blind followers because his mother did not build his character. He has to follow the leaders, because alone, weak, without any protection, easily impressionable, scared of threat, he has to obey the chief. If not, he could be the next victim of the system. Does he have the intention of following the laws of the street? Does this American child have someone to help him confront this fragile existence? As I said, the last time he begged his mother to visit the school in order to ask a counselor, or a school official to give him a particular attention, she did not go.

When he becomes a teenager, Antwann is scared—too young to die, too young to be part of the network of death. Too young to die, for not even tasting the delights of life or for not even fulfilling his mission on earth. Not free to talk. Other members are spying him. He cannot complain. Who is listening to him? Antwann is scared to talk or to breathe too loud. Does he belong to himself? Antwann cannot look in some directions; he has his limits even if he has an apparent freedom.

iii. Apparent Freedom

Seeing this boy holding his house's keys gives me the impression that he is free. Free to be alone in the house. Free to watch any TV show and devote himself to the wrong technological side. In fact, either he is constantly exposed to sex or violence images, or he becomes obese due to a constant consumption of funny food while spending a whole day sitting to watch TV. With a feeble mind, easily influenceable by these perverted shows, there also is every chance that he will begin to try them too early.

Sadly, he is living an apparent freedom that ties him to the dangerous influence of the media. Because at a young age, he is left alone like an abandoned dog in the cold; nobody to lead him, no one to explain to him the real life, no one to share with him the dangers and the consequences of certain acts.

iv. A Loving and Compassionate Boy

Antwann's heart contains love, "this noble sentiment that whoever ignores it is not living" (Lavi Nou Yòk, Theodore Beaubrun, Languichat Debordus). In fact, on many occasions, he has manifested this feeling through his acts.

Sometimes to calm the tension inside the bus, I have to switch him. If I yell, he never despises me; he never frowns; he never hits his fist against the window, never drops his bag, or steps strongly on the floor in a sign of protestation. When I move him, he stays quietly in his new seat until he arrives at his stop. Oftentimes, Antwann fights on the bus as many boys do. I used to fight also when I was a boy. During the time I drove that boy, I have made an observation: Antwann, the biggest passenger on my bus, never hits a friend too hard or in any vital body part. He always looks for their backs. He is not a sadist. Moreover, as any child, immediately after a fight, he begins to talk again to his friends. Given his size for his age, Antwann represents, for the other students on the bus and for the little ones, a big brother who shows affection, compassion, tenderness, and love.

Ready to serve, he does not care sacrificing himself to please his friends. This strong boy likes the other kids. When inside the bus, he is happy, he is laughing, he enjoys the other children's presence. Funny, jovial, he has an innocent face that draws a natural rictus that hides his funny side. With an immaculate face, a naive look, and a perfect smile, he has all that there could be good in a human being. He has nothing evil in him, no hard feelings, no idea or desire of vengeance, accepting whatever I say, whatever I decide like a sheep going to the way of death. There is no real difference between Antwann and the other children. He is also a troublemaker.

v. A Troublemaker

Antwann is not a saint. Like any children, he learns his first curse in daycare or kindergarten. He enjoys using the f word, the s word, and so on. He often gives his opinions about some sensible topics. One day, I heard him talking about lesbians.

One afternoon, I warned him to stop walking in the aisle while the bus was moving. For one reason or another, he didn't want to listen to me, so I moved him to the first row behind me next to a first grade boy. Antwann appeared unhappy for sitting next to a first grade who began to tease him.

That situation gave place to an argument between him and the other student, though Antwann never reacted violently to that boy's nuisance. For sure, Antwann would never physically hurt a little one; he is not a coward, but he has other ways to fight them. To this boy who was teasing him, he reacted by using his middle finger.

The upset boy called me, "Roman."

"What?" I responded while looking at the dome mirror.

"Antwann gives me the middle finger."

Antwann, immediately, to defend himself, responded, "It's not true, Roman. I gave him *three* fingers."

I tried to keep a serious face, but I could not contain myself from bursting out loudly. Anytime I remember these funny moments, I laugh.

vi. One Bad Day

I needed to laugh, but sometimes Antwann and the other students make me angry. We, as school bus drivers, should be able to control our anger even in difficult situations. Some days are out of the spectrum of our will; in other words, some days, trying to completely control a bus with students is a difficult parameter to handle.

In light of such consideration, one day, I reported Antwann and three other boys for misbehaving. They were horse playing, fighting, jumping on the seats and running in the aisle. I was really mad that day. Nonetheless, when I remembered that I was in contact with children, I tried in vain to regain my smiley face. I wanted to run, but if I did, that face would follow me. A kind of shadow covered it. From my pocket, I pulled my handkerchief and wiped my face. Then I looked in the dome mirror; the same angry and mean face looked back at me. In vain, I tried to smile, but I could not. I raised my eyebrows; my face was still cynical. At the same time, I was wondering about a thousand things: my future, my retirement, my goals, my mission in this life. Suddenly, one idea came in my mind; I repeated to myself, "Roman, you'll have to work hard, babe!" Indeed, if every ride were smooth, all children were always quiet, all conditions ideal, and all the measures of safety inside and outside the bus *ceteris paribus*, then the money would be too easy to make. I laugh at myself!

That is what changed and brought a ray of light to my face that morning.

This is a way to tell that the contradictions encountered during a lifetime contribute to the basic beauty of this life. We need to learn to face its challenges and even its insurmountable difficulties. Isn't that fragile life a daily mathematic book of problems and pains? Therefore, we need to learn to find good solutions and cures for each bad day we are living. "What we agree with leaves us inactive, but contradiction makes us productive" (Johann Wolf von Goethe).

vii. The Assistant Principal

The next morning, the assistant principal came to greet the students while they were getting off the bus. She talked to a little girl walking down the bus about her behavior. Behind that girl came Antwann; with her arm, she stopped him.

Looking at me, she said, "How is he doing?"

"Fine," I replied.

Let us make it clear. In some circumstances, we don't have to be a traitor to our students; we report something we can prove.

The assistant principal began to talk to Antwann who didn't say a word. The expression of his eyes let me perceive that he was not happy. With a soft voice, she continued, "Antwann, what's the matter?"

No response.

Perhaps that female assistant principal, who symbolizes beauty, represented an alma mater for all the little Antwanns in the school. All children would feel attracted by her natural charm and her sinuous grace. Another Mona Lisa, her fresh smile gives to the word *school* its true meanings: game, love, security, happiness. Let us wish in the school, she replaces Antwann's mother to talk to him, to give him confidence, to show him how to cross the long journey that leads to the right path of success, to put in his mind a shield that would protect him against the dangers of the world, to build his conscience and his character so that when he will be alone at home, in the school, and later in life he knows what to touch, what to watch, and how to tactfully approach the life so that he does not fall in the complex trap of life.

Antwann characterizes a child who is left to himself. Desertion, negligence, abuse, exploitation, trauma, and so on, are the words that translate his reality of life. The next time a school bus passes in front of our house, we should think and look twice inside the school bus to see if we can read those words in the eyes of one Antwann in pursuit of justice and truth, and craving for tenderness and love. Antwann is looking at us, and each time he looks, he wants to send a message: "Take me with you because I've no one to protect me."

He does not ask for too much. He does not ask for materials; he does not want nice sneakers, expensive cell phones, and designer clothes. What does he want? He just wants us to do our best, to open our arms to greet him, to replace his reckless parents, and to give him the protection he deserves so that the marginal, the perverted, the ones the system tolerates or creates do not take advantage of him as an innocent child. On the contrary, if we turn our back to him, to paraphrase Gregory Peck, Antwann can later become "a villain who will surprise society by his willingness to live by no rules other than his own," (Daily News, June 27, 2011).

CHAPTER XXVIII

Relation Bus Driver-Students

i. Fact

One afternoon, a boy who was walking in the Candlewood Middle School parking lot, said to one of my students, "This driver is mean. He never talks to us."

Basically, this statement lets us understand that, due to the short time of the run and the complexity of the job, the relation between school bus drivers and students is limited to simple look or simple smile; our dialogue is reduced to brief salutations, simple words, sometimes no words. You would say that no real interaction takes place between us and the students. But what can happen during the loading-unloading time or during the trip? Can we, as people, interact and talk about important matters during this time?

ii. Fighting with Students

In February 2008, during a winter recess, I was watching the news when they broadcasted an event. The event was about a fight between a bus driver and a student.

In the same way, in 1979, a strange event happened in my secondary school in Port-au-Prince, the Lycee Toussaint Louverture. During my second year in the school, a teacher received the beating of his life for having been too mean and too arrogant vis-a-vis his students in "4^{ieme}" (equivalent to eighth grade).

What happened?

Pedro, a history teacher, has been beaten for history. After having a virulent dispute with a class that was misbehaving, the next day he brought his karate license and threatened the students. "If anyone dares touch me, I'll beat him up."

As circumstances dictate Pedro, the history teacher, on the contrary, has been beaten by a whole class. With a bruised face, he has been humiliated, belittled, and reduced in front of the other students as a victim boxer after a bloody fight. Come on, Pedro! Instead of teaching the historic events, they have made of you a present event that needs to be taught. The referee of the game became the victim. Therefore, in a fight where he had zero chance to win, Pedro fell KO on the floor.

As a matter of fact, the students set a trap for him. That day during a test, he was beaten up not by one or two students, but by a whole class. That day, the shepherd of the flock has been devoured by the sheep. Contradiction! The rats had reason over the cat. Nature was against him. Did he measure the weight of his act and the excess of his insolence? Pedro "has been counterproductive, because he manifested his personal force; he forced conflict" (George J. Thompson, PhD., Verbal Judo, p. 125). As a victim, he suffered the logical consequences of his arrogance. For causing such a vile act, he felt that he would live with the saddest shame of his life.

At that time, being a teenager, I embraced this vile and shameful act with the eyes and the understanding of a teenager. In other words, I enjoyed its funny side. Now, every day being around teenage students on the bus, that sad example, my experience, and the refreshers course taught me how to tactfully manage any incidents or conflicts with them and, that way, to keep myself from being the laughing stock of the riders.

iii. Do Not Enter This Dead-End

I am going to say something that might shock some school bus drivers. For me in particular, I feel it is improper for any driver to keep, for a long time, an argument with a student, since other school officials are better placed and better prepared to deal with these fragile and delicate situations. In support of that view, we just have to report the problem even if sometimes there is no follow-up.

Nevertheless, school bus drivers can be harassed by students who get easily irritated or students who have behavioral problems, are sick, or are drug addicted or ex-convicted. The law is clear about our reaction in these extreme cases. "In the extreme case of an abnormal student, only for 'protecting himself from physical injury' should a driver use reasonable physical force (8 NYCRR 19.5 [a][i]).

But let us say we are driving a bus where everybody inside is normal and all the conditions being equal, no one would harass us unless we have been mean (make sure we are not!) to them or verbally aggressive with them, and unless we have crossed the limits.

In fact, I have been in a situation where a female student harassed me (A Bizarre Girl Ref. p.37). Her rude reaction called for an answer. Perhaps, either she thought nature was against her (for not having an attractive silhouette, which is something of relative importance), or she was a victim of the society; probably she has been exposed to bully, or she has been raised by her parents amidst total indifference, or she has even been under the influence of drugs or liquors.

An afternoon she was arguing with a boy, and because her speech crossed the bounds of tolerance, I warned her vehemently. Evidently, she was very angry and almost devoured me. Indeed, that student was twisting her right hand near my face as she approached me. She began to insult me and, in a rage of fury, became so close to me that some of her droplets of saliva stroke my face. You would say she wanted to hit me. Why?

Because at that time, it was my first year driving a school bus. Instead of empathizing with her, I confronted her rude behavior, making it more difficult for her to comply. I did not deal with that case with dexterity, calm, and any will to help her instead.

Therefore, any situation that can raise an argument with a student should be shunned. I think it is perverted and wrong for any school bus driver to fight with a student. Anyone who falls in this dead-end reduces and belittles his personality.

iv. The Lack of Experience

"Experience masters everything," said Julius Caesar. Due to lack of experience, full of prejudice and complex, and having a wrong and biased conception of the American teenager, I reacted violently to a violent situation. On the contrary, our reaction needs to be simple in those tough moments: cool down! Cool down any time a student is angry, any time a subaltern, a coworker, our wife is angry.

Remember, stay cool. The more time we spend driving students, the more experience we acquire to absorb their turmoils and their stirs. Therefore, we become, for our passengers, a model who can act and talk calmly in any tense moment; therefore, we control our instincts and our anger. A lack of experience can lead us to absurd acts, whose chain of consequences we will have to face is long. We will pay for our mistakes. If we fight with somebody or, in the worst of the cases, with a student, we will have to drive long distance and spend days in court, to pay a lawyer, to skip job without pay. We can be discharged from the job and even be sentenced to go to jail.

v. A Pact of Unity with Our Students

In my hometown in Port-au-Prince, I heard a sad story about a husband who died a morning while sleeping next to his wife. For being too angry after the last night argument, he did not want to beg her for help. Resentment, what a shame! For me, my wife knows that any time I lay on the bed, I forget everything. We become friends. It is our pact.

It is the same for a child or a student. They have a tacit pact with us. As a school bus driver, a mother, a father, a friend, or even if we never had a child or never lived with a child, the company has taught and still teaches us during the refreshers to learn to transcend ourselves and somewhat walk in their shoes. They do not have to understand us, we should teach them how to understand us, and yet it is necessary for us to understand them.

As a citizen of the world, we should learn to live with people and not wait for people to learn to live with us. As George Bernard Shaw states, "The reasonable man adapts himself to the world; the unreasonable one persists in trying to adapt the world to himself." In support of that view, "we should get rid of our ego…and take pride that, as a school bus driver, we can talk the talk of the children" (Verbal Judo, George J. Thomson, PhD, p. 114), then we will discover how fun this job is.

More than forty students are sitting behind us. Be an example! What is more striking when in situation to fight, we humiliate ourselves; in situation to yell, we use a low pitch voice; in situation to frown, we smile. Such a way of acting gives us control of our students. In return, they will care and feel more sensitive to us; they will apologize to us and respect us. They are children, thus much younger and more inexperienced than us. Try to understand our differences with them. Ask ourselves this question: "How long have I been living with my little brother, sister, or cousin?" Some loud, acid, and acerbic disputes have been raised between us; some fights have even taken place, but we forgot everything and continued playing after. Because something that is stronger than us, that tacit pact, united us.

The same way, a kind of unity with the ones behind us, our students or our passengers, is necessary. We should force ourselves and find a way to draw the students closer to us. Never forget that if something is happening to us, such as a danger, an unexpected event, a heart attack, if we fainted behind the steering wheel, the students, our friends will be the first ones to secure the bus and to call 911 for help. Therefore, we should give them a good reason to do so.

vi. Texting Behind the Wheel

Most American teenagers are spinning in a technologic cycle, where every three to six months, they have to change their new electronic devices in order to pace with the exigencies of the time. Nowadays, teenager and adolescent students embrace the new trend, which makes it more convenient to text on the phone than to talk. Even some adults with snobbish attitude fall also in this cyclic trap. A close observation on the roads shows that many drivers are texting while driving.

In this context, in May 2010, the New York media made a big noise about a school bus driver who, in violation with the 49CFR 383, 384, 390, 391, 392 of the FMCSA, was snapped by a student while texting and driving. The elementary student passenger forwarded the picture right away to her parents. Consequently, after twenty years on the job, that driver has been fired without further ado.

vii. Questions

In fact, considering the risk taken by that driver and also by many others to read, text, and drive, people are entitled to ask a few questions. Has that student been bullied, made fun of, or verbally abused (children never forget verbal abuse) by the driver? Or did the driver allow a kind of sloppiness on the bus where that child has been offended by other peers? Or has she observed the driver texting every day behind the steering wheel, and therefore report that wrong and sinister behavior to her parents who probably have asked her obvious facts in order to request disciplinary actions from the company? Or was she scared to die too early and decided by herself to take the driver's picture?

Here are so many questions that only the bus driver and the student are fit to bring a bit of light to clear the situation. What is clear is, as a professional driver, she took the wrong and dangerous option of texting behind the steering wheel, forcing then the company to give her a dose of her own medicine.

viii. Confession

"Roman, did you ever text while driving a school bus?"

"Never."

On many occasions, I have talked on the phone in my car or on the bus— if there's no student—while driving. In the case students are on board, if I can hear the phone's vibrations, whenever possible at the next stop, I quickly look at the phone to verify if it is not a call from the company. Anytime the call relates to my duty, I pulled over. Other times, I have been tempted to look at some phone numbers (a distraction) while the bus was moving. Now, I get rid of that bad habit.

Did the girl's parents who called ever talk, text, and drive while in his car?

As I said before, in some situations, the job requires zero tolerance. Therefore, any drivers who do not respect the conditions and create justifiable reasons will be dismissed.

ix. Communication

A student on my bus, Kimberly, daughter of a school bus driver who is working for another school bus company, has been switched, on different occasions, to the seat located behind me for emotional and disruptive behavior. A few months later, that troublemaker matured throughout the year to finally become a growing girl and a valid helper. Day after day, she understood me better. She understood the safety requirements inside the bus: just sit down so you do not distract the bus driver's attention.

To reinforce my point, let me explain to you what happened on the bus one morning. The district just added to my run one more stop on Vanderbilt Parkway near High School East. I stopped to pick up the students: a boy and a girl. After getting on the bus, the girl sat down quietly; the brother didn't want to sit down; he was kneeling on the seat. And in order to talk, he turned to look at his friend who was himself sitting. I looked at him through the dome mirror, a way to tell him to sit down. The other day, I warned him and explained to him the reasons he had to sit down while the bus was in motion. So anytime our eyes met, anytime we shared a look, we were supposed to understand each other, like father and son. This time, lost in an interesting conversation, he could not see me anytime I raised my head to warn him.

Kimberly understood what was in my mind. She turned to the boy's sister, who was sitting next to her and said, "What's your brother's name?"

The sister murmured some words that she probably did not hear. With a firm tone, her voice loud, she shouted, "Tell your brother, whatever his name is, to sit down, because he is not allowed to stand up while the bus is moving." The boy obeyed her and sat down immediately.

Happy and proud of her, I thanked her for being an efficient support of communication.

x. Joke

Inside a public bathroom, a heavyweight American boxer meets a Haitian man who is talking Creole on the phone. The boxer warns the Haitian man, "Get the f…k out of my way. Stop talking this funny patois, f…g Haitian."

The Haitian man does not understand English. He does not have any idea that the boxer is serious. So he smiles and replies, "Yeah, sir."

"The French brought you here to fight in the war of Savannah. The war is over. Go back to your f…n country. Get out now or I kill you."

"Yeah," answers the Haitian, covering his mouth (he is missing three teeth) and laughing. He thinks the man is telling a joke.

"So you think it's funny. I'm going to teach you a lesson," the boxer says while moving close to him and grinding his teeth.

My brother Haitian, while laughing, says "Oh yeahhh!"

The boxer hits him. He lost two other teeth and fell down KO on the floor.

Evidently, my compatriot uses very few words to communicate. Being in an uncomfortable and confused situation, he just smiles and answers yeah. And quite surprisingly, so many times, I just said yeah in confused dialogues with little children, with other migrants and even with some born and uneducated Americans. In general, the American people, contrary to the boxer, are tolerant and patient when dialoguing with migrants who do not own the English language. For sure, they will not hit us if we answer yeah to any confused question. As for me, until now, I still do not mind laughing without covering my mouth!

xi. Communication Difficulties

Sincerely, I admire the tolerance and the patience of the American people who always take time to understand us even when we connect words that do not make sense. Every day, I also imagine how difficult it is for the American children to understand some migrant school bus drivers. I still have memories of Suffolk Community College, where I used to pronounce some words in a funny way that sometimes made the students laugh at me. Normal. In the same context, another day, two employees of the Huntington Station Public Library laughed at me after a funny *lapsus linguae* escaped from my mouth. In fact, I wanted a piece of paper; but I asked, "Can I have a piece of sheet?" You get it!

They laughed at me until they cry.

Truly, in the transportation system, one of the biggest problems encountered by migrant school bus drivers with students is communication. There is every chance that the ones who moved to the USA in their thirties have experienced this problem. To me in particular, I still, even now (after nine years in America), face difficulties understanding right away some heavily accented comments made by many American adults, for there are words, slangs, idiomatic expressions, and questions that I still have difficulty captivating the essence right away.

It is also important for us to think twice before using a word in the context, or interpreting it otherwise. Sometimes we acquiesce or smile to a threat or an insult and wrongly say all right in a situation where we otherwise have to say no.

xii. The Brennan Middle School Boy

On my first day on the job working as a school bus monitor for another company, I had an argument with a boy from Brennan Middle School. We picked up the boy in Huntington Station. He entered the school van and dropped all his body on the seat. From the corner of his eye he gave me, the unknown, a dirty look, since he knew that my duty was to warn him, to report his behavior, and to shape him my way or the way the transportation system wishes.

I looked back at him. I waited three minutes to see if he was in compliance with the safety standards. That day, I could wait forever. He was moving on the seat.

It was time for action.

I was naïve to think that I could convince that nut student with a few connected words in my stony accent. In fact, with a biased and preconceived idea of the task allowed to me, I repeated my first famous words on duty: "Sit down and put your seatbelt on."

The boy didn't even glance at me.

Since it is recommended by the NHTSA and, in a state of anger, I shouted, "You *must* sit down and put your seatbelt on."

The driver, a retired Greek, looked through the dome mirror, then smoothly told me, "Leave him alone, Roman. That's fine."

In a sign of victory, the boy despised me.

I shut my mouth.

New (only a month in America) on the job, I didn't captivate, understand, and weigh the context of the verb *must*. In essence, *must* indicates an obligation: he was forced to sit down, as if I was pushing his shoulder down to force him to sit down. *Must* also expresses, in this context, my irritation, though the child was calm. Basically, I wanted to impose my rule, my personality, and in brief, my ego instead of looking for the purpose (moving on the bus is a kind of distraction), the goal (reach the school safely), and the consequences (a report, lose the privilege of the bus, walk to school). I used the commanding style in action, whose motto is, "Do it because I say so" (Daniel Coleman, Primal Leadership p.76). In short, it was a classic recipe for dissonance. As a result I created conflict, which gives me less power over that boy. Consequently, that day, he never put the seatbelts on. I was KO for threatening him with such anger.

Later, we became friends. I even took picture of him. Thanks to the power of communication.

Communication is one of the most important tools in the relation children-bus drivers. To paraphrase an author, "Our tongue is a lion. If we attach him, he'll look at us. If we let him escape, he'll devour us." So control our instinct before we talk. We must learn to use our language more skillfully. Children often react the way we act—with manner if we have good manner, violent if we act violently. Children are like mirrors, which reflect the beam of light projected on them with even more brightness and more intensity.

xiii. A Violent Case

To illustrate a violent child's reaction resulting from his mother's abuse, here is what happened years ago in Haiti.

One afternoon, a boy Jerome had a brawl with his sister Regina. The mother Lotida interfered in the fight, and to separate them, she only hit the boy. By mistake, Lotida's finger entered inside the boy's mouth. Do not ask me what happened! In pain, she begged her son to stop biting her. Surely he stopped, but he already damaged the mother's finger.

To defend himself against the mother in fury, he said he thought that the finger was his sister's.

In sum, communication is not only a tool, but a way to appease people's fear, people's anger. School bus drivers should be open-minded people. To face the complexity of life here, we school bus drivers keep an apparent distance from the students. Many reasons explain that: fear of a lawsuit, short time spent with students, etc. We should never forget that we are dealing with children. We should also use our common sense; take risk anytime we feel it is necessary to talk to a child, as long as we do not say anything uncalled for.

When we stop at the elementary school, the little ones tend to come by us and ask us all kinds of questions. In order to understand their context, we need to do a tough cerebral work. Let us hope that one day, the concerned authorities will include in the refreshers some Intercultural-Communication Seminars for the immigrant school bus drivers who do not own the language.

xiv. The Use of Word

A few passages of the book of Georges J. Thompson, PhD will help explain how difficult it is for a migrant school bus driver to control the reality inside the school bus. Before here is what happened to me in 2002.

One morning, I was on duty as a door guard in a store at Carl Place's Shopping Center. A customer fell down because her feet were entangled in a piece of plastic that was dropped on the floor.

I chuckled to myself and walked toward her in a sign of sympathy. For sure, I was looking in my mind for something nice to say. (Today, I would quickly ask her, "Are you OK?") The lady was in a rage since she was in pain. Thinking that I wanted to make fun of her, she exploded, "Are you laughing at me? Do you know I can sue you?" (Almost everyone dreams to win of a bogus lawsuit here in America.)

What was my problem to smile in such a sad situation?

Simple. That morning I could not find, in real time, the right word to relieve her. In fact, we suffer from a lack of word, a communication gate that stopped many of us, migrant drivers, in our interactions with our passenger students. Moreover, we lack one indispensable tool George J. Thomson, PhD. presents to achieve our objective when communicating with students—"the use of words with maximum effectiveness and maximum effort."

Indeed, most foreign drivers over thirty who migrate to the USA from a country where English is not an official language confront difficulties to use the right word anytime they need it. They should practice and study English to gain the ability to find the right words, use, and connect them in texts and contexts that make sense and are effective and efficient to persuade the students to cooperate.

xv. The Art to Speak: A Headache for Migrant Drivers

Read this statement from a disabled child, "I can't remember the frustration of not being able to speak. I knew what I wanted to say, but I couldn't get the word out, so I would just cry."

We, as migrant school bus drivers, find ourselves sometimes in this sad situation. We need some expressions, set phrases, and some clichés to help us better communicate and persuade our students to do what we want them to do on the bus. Basically, it is a challenge for us to generate voluntary compliance. We hardly make it happen, since we do not own the language. In consequence, for that reason doubled with the lack of a spontaneous oral volubility, many migrant drivers have been switched to other routes. And even some fluently speaking English drivers have lost their regular routes under the parents' complaints for not having the art to speak or to persuade the students to become more cooperative.

xvi. Translation

According to Professor George J. Thomson's definition, "Translation is the ability to put what we say in the most proper, fitting, assertive, and powerful words possible."

It was quite a problem for me interacting with the students during my first year in the job. In fact, while I was trying to convince a girl to sit down, she closed my mouth with a legitimate commentary to her friend. "What did he say? This driver has a funny accent."

With my funny accent, my stony accent (it sounds like I have a stone in my mouth), I couldn't even pronounce the words the right way to express my idea. So how could I translate it to her? Noise disturbed the message and interfered with the reception, so the message couldn't go five out of five. It was biased, and the receiver couldn't catch the true and precise meaning in his mind.

Therefore, a bad translation can lead to a wrong interpretation with sad and disastrous consequences. A stress on a wrong syllable or a bad punctuation sign can reverse the meaning of a phrase, which can cause the translation to become fatal. Look how fatal this order of a general to a soldier was. The general said, "Grace, pas fusiller (Grace, not kill). The soldier wrote: "Grace pas, fusiller (Grace not, kill)."

As an evident deduction, the prisoner was killed. He was killed because the words were not translated the right way in the soldier's mind. It is the same for students anytime they do not understand us; they interpret our message their way.

Finally, it is important to realize how complex and tough it is for us, immigrant drivers, to interact with our passengers. Some of us, conscious of the problem, have attended English school to learn to better communicate. Other *violent* drivers never studied English. (Please allow me, dear reader, to give other meanings to the adjective *violent*: improvised, bold, audacious, in search of the unknown; people in this category applies the theory of Georges-Jacques Danton: To survive in America, "we need to dare, to dare again, always to dare!") They just catch or learn to connect some words. That way, they put the fragile and smart American students between fires. In their dialogue, these drivers sometimes risk to mix two different and incompatible verbal chemicals, whose reaction can lead to an explosion in the American linguistic lab.

Such translations confuse the students and transport them in such a state where they dream of being in the Tower of Babel.

xvii. A Tribute to a Driver

It is important to manifest to the children what we feel in words and deeds. On morning, I covered a route; and because some elementary students were misbehaving, I took the microphone to calm them. And after talking to them, I concluded saying, "I love you."

At the school, while those students were leaving, a girl stopped by my chair and surprisingly said, "Do you really love us?"

"Surely," I answered.

I have seen van drivers who have very close connection with students who ride their vans. But in my experience as a school bus driver, I have never seen students so connected to a big bus driver.

I met one Haitian big bus driver named Jude in October 2006 in a middle school. I was doing Route 439 at that time. One day, he parked next to my bus in Otsego Elementary school. Immediately, as he was pulling in, all the students on my bus were ecstatic and happy to see him. They were screaming, jumping, standing on the seats to greet Jude, to call his name, and talk to him. His intense voice covered all the children's voices. He reminded me of Odilon, a Haitian teacher whose voice used to fill the entire Haitian Faculty of Sciences Auditorium. His presence created inside my bus a deafening noise that was difficult to control. With a high-pitched and a celestial voice, Jude saluted the children. "How you doing, guys?"

I immediately recognized his accent; the French-Creole accent, my accent.

And the happy students never stopped repeating, "Jude, Jude, Jude."

Everywhere, on every seat, I heard, "Jude, Jude." Truly, I can feel that euphoria, that contentment, which manifests in the child when the mother comes home after work. I murmured, "Wow! This driver is wonderful."

For us who drive a school bus, Jude should be our model in a certain way. Like me, this man is Haitian, and his third language is English. But with his tongue, he has the magic to transcend people's heart. This man should be our model because he is always smiling, always joking, and always finds something nice to say. Contrary to many other drivers, he reaches another dimension, which makes him closer to the students.

Besides, during my first months, the students took the habit to ask me, "Are you Jude?" Perplexed, I questioned myself, "Why even after giving them my name, they kept calling me Jude?" Why? Now I understand the reason. Jude used to do this route; Jude has touched their subconscious, perhaps making them dreaming of him during the night.

What a caring, wonderful, and happy school bus driver he is. Chapeau pou ou, frèm! (I give you the hat, brother!)

Continue your noble duty; continue this way and your work will be great. Continue this noble mission in loving and protecting those little angels with a clear conscience; you will benefit of the blessings of God.

Respects!

CHAPTER XXIX

A Clear Conscience

i. Fact

After the earthquake, I visited my devastated country Haiti. The second day, I met up with my longstanding friend Dominique. We spent four years studying together in INAGHEI (National Institute of Administration, Management and International High Studies). After the earthquake, he was the one I asked the next day to check the safety of all my family members living in the capital. Immediately after, he took his motorcycle to face the aftershocks and the cadavers and to give me the first news about my parents living in Port-au-Prince. At that time, he was in charge of a primary school in the city of Delmas, Port-au-Prince. Here is what happened to him one day.

One Saturday morning, he mistakenly hit another car whose passengers were the driver, his wife, and two students from his school. The father verbally lanced some obscenities to my friend who never argued with him. Since he was at fault, he calmly told him, "Sir, I'm deeply sorry. The car is material vanity. Just do an estimate and I'll give you a check."

Strangely, while their father was arguing with Dominique, both children run to hug my friend.

Their father, who could not believe his eyes, began to question his wife about the children's reaction. He wrongly suspected his wife of having a kind of relation with my friend. He was not aware that Dominique was running the school his children attended. In reality, nothing was going on. What was going on was the position my friend holds in the children's lives.

Normally, children look elsewhere for others to fill the empty part of their lives and help them answer thousands of questions in their minds. Perhaps Dominique answers their questions. Is he is a shadow of love who spreads the word of happiness for the children? Is he a kind of comfort and a beam of affection for them? Does he complete the lack of understanding these children miss at home? Only his conscience can guide him.

ii. Guidelines of a Clear Conscience

A clear conscience would lead the world to a better direction. That gold rule should be all school bus drivers' motive in the accomplishment of their task. A clear conscience appeals us to a better sense of duty. Otherwise, we need to fulfill our mission as good and perfect as it can be. We need to do everything in the best possible way and give the best of ourselves to please the children. Therefore, people who cannot answer the above mentioned questions are doing the wrong job. An asthmatic cannot be a house cleaner; the same people who do not get along with children should not adventure themselves in this complicate domain of driving a school bus. People who easily lose patience and are unable to work in noisy environment should not drive students. Those who cannot deal with some surprises should not drive handicapped students, because one day or another, they will have to face a kind of surprise on the bus.

Not too long ago, a colleague driver, who got fired after two at-fault accidents, gave his testimony to another driver, "The high school students are going to be happy when they get the news." Dealing with students requires patience. Do not be like that driver who showed me his ID and told me, "I'm a retired police officer. I'm going to deal with them. No noise, no talking, no chewing gum, no eating, no standing on the bus. Clear the aisles and hands between their legs."

Oh! Oh! You should put chains in their legs also. Are they slaves or prisoners?

I did not see him the next day. I never see him again.

Children are flexible like the willow tree and graceful like a cat; they can survive strong winds and create ways to quickly escape danger. We cannot break them. If we are too weak, they take advantage of us; too mean, they tease us or even retaliate (Remember what happened to Pedro, the history teacher, Ref. p. 176). Therefore, dealing with them requires suppleness and firmness, because I am pretty sure a heavyweight lies on the conscience of whoever acts mean and inhuman with students.

iii. A Mean and Inhuman Case

A particular cruel case, that touches my heart, deserves to be pointed out. It was a morning of winter, March 3, 2010, a dispatcher ordered me to bring some harnesses to James E. Allen, Jr./Sr. Arriving at the school, I witnessed a crazy situation where all the buses were ready and parked in the school, though many students were still waiting on the sidewalk to get boarded. Was it a lack of planning or any other problem because the buses appeared not to have enough place to fit all the wheelchair students available?

In such a circumstance, as an employee, I decided to help the teachers find seats inside the vans. Indeed, I looked through the windows of some vans; thus, I convinced some drivers to get more students on their bus, or to move other wheelchair students who could walk to get a regular seat inside the van and create space for the ones who cannot walk to the bus. Many drivers cooperated, and almost all the students fitted in the buses and the vans. But a particular student was despised because, according to the testimony of one driver, most of the drivers categorically refused to drive her under the pretext that she was too noisy.

What a shame!

That handicapped girl was outside in the cold, waiting for a good Samaritan driver, who had space to ride her to that charter in Garden

City. One teacher was begging me to find a place to put her so that she can enjoy the moment with the others.

I decided to double-check. Finally, I found a van that, with a capacity to fit four wheelchairs (three on the driver's side, one on the door side next to the lift), only contained two wheelchairs inside. The space near the door could not fit a chair because they have filled with glue the holes that hold the belt, probably for safety reasons, being too close to the lift door. The space in the back (driver's side) was OK. After a long debate with the van driver, I finally convinced her to board the child. Against herself, she decided to open the door and lift the student on the van.

When the student was inside, the driver's assistant (DA) argued with me that he could not put the straps in the back left angle of the van. I said, "OK, I'm going to do it."

So I kneeled to do it.

I tried to move forward the two wheelchairs in the front to create more space. Both the DA and the driver did not want me to move them. I did not move them! I said, "All right."

My first job was a driver's assistant, so I used to put the straps in corner. I did the second strap, the front left corner behind the second wheelchair. Now, I told the driver's assistant to buckle the two right wheels, since he was sitting and looking at me putting the straps. Wasn't it his job? He refused categorically, pretending that he cannot fit in the aisle to put the belts.

In my mind, I said, "Wow! This guy is playing with his job." (It was the time of the recession in America.)

Did he forget that this is a new America and his reaction could be subject to a warning and even dismissal? Should the company lose a contract because of our laziness or our indifference in the job?

He never tried. He did not even touch the belts. He just stayed at a certain distance and told me that the chair cannot fit in the space the manufacturer has conceived and done for the chair. Dear coworker, we are living in America, a country with smart, gifted, and bold people who can transform impossible into possible. Human beings would not explore the moon if they had never tried? Was he scared of taking risk? "It is not necessary to do great things; we just need to try" (Edgar La Selve). He wrongly followed his laziness and, consequently, risked his job. Did he just need the money without doing anything? My friend, this is bad faith, unconcern, and lack of sense of responsibility.

I wanted to complete the task; in fact, I put the third belt. When the driver saw that I was determined and about to put the last one, she jumped from her seat and shouted, "You know what, this is my bus. (Perhaps she bought it with her money.) I'm not going to drive this bus with three wheelchairs."

"OK," I calmly replied.

I left the van without arguing back. (I didn't want to be wrongly accused since my duty in the company is to drive) Then I called my operations manager to explain the situation.

The driver went out, opened the lift door, and dropped the innocent and passive girl on the curbside in the cold.

The driver's assistant, whose hand could not fit the angles to reach and tight the belts with the wheels, can now fit to unbuckle them. What a contrast; what a paradox!

By the way in Haiti, I heard a joke about an armless man who was accused of stealing of bag of flour. At the court, the man begged the judge's pity and convinced her that it is materially impossible for him to lift the bag, since he does not have any arms. After considering that palpable fact, the judge freed him and gave him the bag of flour.

The armless man waited until everyone was gone; then he leaned the bag on his right calf, heeled it, gave it an *uchi mata*, and dropped it on his right shoulder.

Upon which, the judge ordered to put him in jail.

What was the verdict for that driver and her assistant? Let's allow the free will to decide.

Our decisions do not ask us to put the students' life in jeopardy. But was it a problem putting that poor girl on the bus? What kind of human these people are? I am sure during the night, the free will has warned them for that fault. For sure, any supervisor or manager who was in the vicinity would have sanctioned these two lazy employees.

In the end, we cannot just like the money and hate the job. In America, no matter what job we do—manual, technical, intellectual, conceptual, etc.—we get paid on Fridays a check that is equivalent of dollar bills that only have Washington's picture in them.

iv. The Eyes of our Conscience

One morning, on my way to St. Anthony High School, I pass the Fire House on Eatons Neck Road. A few feet ahead, I observe an elderly woman walking in the street. Each step translates a kind of dissonant move that shows she takes great pain to walk. You would say that her squelettal mechanism needs to be lubricated. I proceed eastbound on Asharoken Road, Northport; the yellow sun hits my mirror like a flame of fire and tells me, "Good morning. I'm ready for the daily concert."

I have witnessed countless sunrises, but I never watch any with such a clear and licit message. In fact, in that part of atmosphere, a flock of geese shaping like the letter v is about to make a sea landing on the blue portion of ocean between the North Shore of Long Island and Connecticut; a few miles over the towers of the Long Island Power Authority, a plane is crossing. And from its engines escapes a white horizontal line on the infinite blue sky; the heavy smoke coming out of the towers draws a curious image where I perceive from the distance a hand pointing its index finger straight to my bus.

While looking at this wonderful spectacle that nature is offering, that message transports me to a state where I feel at the same time a feeling of happiness and sadness invading me. I am happy because it awakens all my senses for I just drank a cup of coffee; probably the blood flow has already crossed all the circuits in my brain. And I feel sad because the message is written in golden words, and it translates the real and painful life stories of thousands of innocent children on earth, victims of our meanness. Indeed, my inspiration doubles; and at the same time, I begin to hum the lyrics of an engaged Haitian artist's song. The cool morning breeze of the shore transports the words to a melodious tone. From a long distance one can hear:

"Men who are fighting
So that life blossoms,
So that hunger dies,
So that children enjoy
The nice tomorrows that will come."

While singing, I look at the glass that protects me from the glare of the sun; I see four eyes. Stunned, I frown, and I look again. The four eyes look back at me. They remind me of my great-grandmother, who told me a story about me: As a toddler, I saw my picture in a car window while eating a snack. I said to her, "Gran'n (Grandma), he is asking me."

She responded, "Don't worry about him, son."

Probably I see those eyes again, the same eyes that I used to study in the candlelight or under an electric pole in Haiti; the same eyes that had contemplated the marvelous nature, the steps of the clouds, the moon and the stars; eyes, when my body is twisted, let flow the tears of pain, remorse, neglect, loneliness, sadness, human meanness, and selfishness; tears of exploitation of others by others, tears of joy. I see the same eyes that projected, in my youth, hot rays to hypnotize girls and indeed give them a clear interpretation of my sane and bestial intentions.

But wait! Those eyes that are looking at me now are different.

First, they look at me and question me about my fear, my prejudice, my complex, my lies, my indifference, my contempt, my jealousy, my hatred, and my wrong impression toward parents. Those eyes question me about many questions I used to ask myself while doing the job. Do I, without any sense of logic, ever favor some parents to the detriment of others? Or do I ever act or talk rudely to a category of parents while coddling and spoiling many others? Or in the morning, do I blow the horns once I stop in front of this little house, whereas I wait quietly three to five minutes in front of my friend's mansion? Or do I apply the rules to force that pregnant mother to wait at the corner in the cold as required, while entering somebody else's driveway to pick up their children contrary to the left and right sheets?

Those eyes are still looking at me. I am scared!

Secondly, those eyes question me about my contribution to the company—questions relating to the role played by the company in my life: Does it help me or not? Do I ask too much compared to what I receive? Do I give too much or should I give more? In my pursuit of fair treatment and better work conditions, what have I given in return to contribute to the expansion of the company? Do I understand the boss and his team's philosophy? Should I work side by side with other employees for the advancement and the expansion of the company?

For the sake of making hours, do I ever blindly flatter any manager, agree to any insult, or try to please them in a way that other people find unpleasant? Do I ever stab any employee behind his back? Do I wrongly use the company materials? Do I use its vehicles for my personal needs? Do I falsify time sheets to scam the company's money? Do I drive slowly or wait somewhere to justify my time? Do I ever purposely run over a pothole to damage any leaf-spring? For any minor accident, do I ever file any bogus and unfounded lawsuit against the company? Or, pardon me, do I ever have sex with any employee or prostitute in the yard, inside the school bus, or in any office?

I look back; those four eyes still keep looking at me.

Thirdly, those eyes question me deep down about myself. The intensity of our wickedness or the degree of our understanding can transform those eyes into various colors: red, blue, yellow, etc. In fact, these questions test me about my duty. Those four eyes sympathize with the handicapped girl who can only say one phrase to her bus attendant. You would think her tongue is chained to her palate, giving me the feeling that, as a human being, she is constantly living in a world of dream where words cannot come with the same fluidity as when she is awake.

Those eyes keep looking at me for many other reasons. They want to know if I have been good, bad, sincere, or hypocritical toward my students. They ask me if I do not choose deliberately to pass a stop and leave a child behind, if I do not run on purpose over a bump or brake hard to force students to sit down. They ask me if I did not curse any child yesterday. They ask me if I ever wrongly report a child or order sanctions for an innocent student; if I ever adjust my mirrors vertically to contemplate the girls' intimate apparel when they forget themselves and sit down in a way that deviates from the formal norm; if I never make any vulgar comments, ask for private information, show any surge of heart to student; or finally, if I ever intimately involve with any. So many questions they are asking me. I am scared of those eyes. Ahhhh! They are still looking at me. Please stop looking at me. Should I jump, run, or look back at them?

Wait! I am doing fifteen on Asharoken Road. The drivers behind are upset, but do not protest; let me proceed a little faster.

It does not matter how fast we move; we cannot disappear the field of vision of those eyes. The only sure thing is, we will have a clear conscience if we have done our job equitably; if not, we will get the other side of the coin. First, to the company, we, as school bus drivers, need, anytime at work, to arm ourselves with the shield of conscience to perform our tasks and serve for the money that we receive. Then we should not let our petty, biased, and unfounded sentiments stop us from appreciating the parents' good and positive sides. Finally, to the wheelchair bus driver, the next time a poor noisy handicapped girl comes on your van, look at those eyes that represent an echo of your conscience.

We get paid to drive the students. This is our duty. So let us just accomplish it with a clear conscience. Evidently, a clear conscience would dictate us to judge with equity. All equitable judges would only deliver verdicts based on real and rational judgments, because any judge who tilts to one side of the balance will also fall under the weight of his injustice. If he does not fall immediately, his bad and inconsequent verdicts would haunt him everywhere throughout the night of the time.

As proof, read this Socrates' narration written by Platon years ago about justice as honesty in word and deeds. "When the prospect of dying is near at hand, a man begins to feel some alarm about things that never troubled him before…At any rate he is beset with fear and misgiving; he begins thinking over the past: is there anyone he has wronged? If he finds that his life has been full of wrongdoing, he starts up from his sleep in terror like a child, and his life is haunted by dark forebodings; whereas, if his conscience is clear, that 'sweet Hope…' that Pendar speaks of is always with him to tend his age" (The Republic of Plato, Oxford University Press, 1966, p. 6).

CHAPTER XXX

In The Middle Of The Ocean

Alone in the middle of the ocean, I swim in the deep and cold water. Take a second to hear my cry that is tearing the empty and infinite horizon around me. It is a cry for help. Am I self-sufficient to reach the shore? Can I survive the powerful waves that tend to push me back to the depths of the ocean? I would like to touch the shore. The aquatic predators are already aware of my presence as a strange element that disturbs the system. I fear they may be upset. Should I pay for invading their environment?

We, as migrants, have been swimming for so long in the American ocean in pursuit of an unprecise and uncertain goal. We are totally deprived: no sonar, no rudder, no map, no compass, no light to clear the way and direct us to a right and precise destination. Our behavior, our acts, and the nature of our mission would give us a color, a size, and a shape of destiny. Either we fit ourselves as a piece of this social puzzle, giving a sense to this society, or we line up ourselves with the ones living on the margins of society; and ipso facto, our days are counted. Either we are swallowed like plankton or herbs and disappear in a greedy and hungry sea predator's stomach, or we live in a peaceful and respectable coexistence with others. Living is a fight, a fight against predators. I am that fish in the middle of the ocean.

The American ocean is also deep in contradictions, in bad influences, and in quick and dangerous advantages. Living is a choice. Depending on our choice, we could stay in the surface to enjoy everything that completes the nature and makes life ideal, or we could sink in the dark depths until we die. If we are fit and know how to swim and follow the normal and rational waves in our behavior, our acts, and our decisions, we could stay off trouble. In other words, if we stand like a rock, we'll resist every wrong object that sparkles in our eyes and we'll only look on the ocean's side that is deep in opportunities, deep in advantages, deep in resources in its *depths*, and deep in all good things for everyone who needs to live as real people should.

On the contrary, if we decide to follow the extravagant currents, the irrational and ruthlessly ambitious waves, if we become so big that we precariously balance in the water, we would find ourselves inside two opposite currents that would spin us and propulse us to the deep corners of remorse, resignation with the system, even disgust of ourselves. In light of such considerations, the choice is clear: "In matter of style, follow the current; in matter of principle, stand like a rock (Thomas Jefferson)."

There were days that I felt deep down in the ocean. I covered my eyes with a pair of sunglasses in order to clearly observe without the least discomfort the creatures and the greenery inside, but also to hide my worries, my guilt, my fear, my problems and my interior heartbreak. I did not want to let the creatures in the environment around me to perceive the mystery, and I did not want them to worry about me.

i. A State of Resignation

People forget that we could be forced to submerge in the inmost depths of the ocean under some clear circumstances. We need to have courage and tact to swim against the tide and fight back to come on the surface. In this context, various testimonies of this nation's children let me understand that they are living in a state of resignation. In the ocean, they accept some strange situations against their will. Like the music said, "They lead a life without reason to live." They wrongly pretend that life has never smiled to them. You would say an end in itself: "the die is cast" (Julius Caesar). In other words, they have washed their hands.

According to them, nothing can save their skins. They are done. They have given reason to the system. In fact, one American employee told me, his face down and his legs shaking, "Roman, I'm done. There is nothing I can do to get out of this crap."

"I disagree."

"Why?"

"Because you just have yourself to take care. I completely disagree."

Nevertheless, I admire his sincerity, since he did not make up his face with that kind of hypocrisy that kills the system of things here. Like an English teacher told me, "In America, you always answer I'm fine." In other words, some people, in appearance, pretend to be fine, though in essence it is the contrary. They are enchained, and to yield the requirements of the environment, they do not have inner peace. According to Elise miller Davis, "They are living a horrible existence where they are trying to be what they are not."

Anytime I think about that American employee, I smile.

I smile because although America might appear tough for some Americans and some immigrants, for many others, it is another matter. We can go around the nets and swim without being trapped or drowned. In other words, we learn to, "put the bone into the okra" (Fouye zo nan kalalou, Haitian quote). That is to say, we want to blow the smoking piece of wood until we get fire. Like Henry David Thoreau simplifies it in the chapter two of *Walden*, "We want to live deep and suck out all the marrow of life…to drive life into a corner, and reduce it to its lowest terms, and, if it proves to be mean…, and publish its meanness to the world; or if it were sublime…, and be able to give a true account of it" (Walden and Civil Disobedience, Signet Classic, 1999 Pge 72-73).

The instinct of survival has to give a true account of life. In the American ocean, there are different ways to fight to survive. We are shaking, dancing, jumping, running; we even kneel ourselves down to fight this fight of life. Judge us as cowards if we accept a resignation, which is synonym of desperation. In our vocabulary, the word *desperation* has disappeared. Desperation is a curse, since "it is a characteristic of wisdom not to do desperate things" (Henry David Thoreau, Walden and Civil Disobedience, Signet Classic 1999 Pge 5). Sincerely, my friend, America is a beautiful, blessed, great, and rich piece of land, an easy country where any portion of time we take to fly above ourselves to awaken our sense of creativity can bring us success.

ii. Real People Live in this Ocean

In the American ocean, we have met wonderful and real people who not only came up to us with a smile, but also demonstrated their friendship, their support toward us. As a matter of fact, one afternoon an unknown American white man stopped his car twenty feet behind mine with its four-way flashers on to protect me on Deer Park Avenue while I was changing a flat tire. He decided to leave until after the woman sitting next to him began to argue with him and convinced him of the dangerous character of his act. I salute his good intentions. Moreover a white woman invited me to come in her office a cold winter morning on Route 112 while I was waiting for a transit bus.

How many times have we heard the word thanks? In this environment, people cultivate the sense of appreciation. As proof, in December, the parents, while handing us envelopes (with money for sure, some contains one hundred bucks), apologize to us (in their eyes, they think it's nothing), and thank us (for the very little thing we have done). In their mind, they think they should do more. You'd say that they have a feeling of guilt tipping us.

Wow! Thanks, and respects for them.

iii. Stop Pushing Me Down

I have swum hundred miles against violent waves and strong currents to come to the ocean surface, but I feel a hand pushing my head down. Surprisingly, so many cultivated Americans and many others trumpet that Haiti is a slum country as the news lets them believe. It is the same for people who believe that the Africans are running with lions and tigers in the African forests. It is a kind of negligent or unconscious belief in a lie that has been loudly told so many times. Not everyone wants to cultivate the ability of good judgment. Many never criticize the news. For them, even for many intellectual Haitian mercenaries, Haiti our dear country, is a piece of garbage. Indeed, a driver who used to live in Miami testified to me that he thought "all Haitians were drug dealers until he met us in the job."

Yeah! We are robbers, we have the lowest IQ, we brought HIV, and for sure, we are boat people as everyone in the USA is, excluded the Native Americans. History is a cycle. All of us have been spinning inside this cycle a certain time of the times.

To hear them talk, you would say that Haitians have no financial, industrial, cultural, social, human resources etc. Nothing at all, just the voodoo and Cite Soleil (Sun City)! In the second half of the twentieth century, Doctor Jean Price Mars, in his book *So Spoke the Uncle*, has already speculated on the acknowledgement of this indifference, "Problems which concern the behavior of one group of men are sufficient grounds to warrant the indifference of the rest of humanity."

Accordingly, I witnessed, among others, two examples that explain how it is hard for us to swim to the surface.

a) The Skeptical Employee

A coworker expressed his doubts to me about one Haitian employee who told him that he was studying law in Haiti. Listen to what he said. "Roman, is it true the Haitian driver assistant was a law student in Haiti?"

"Yes," I replied.

With an ironic tone and shaking his head negatively, he added, "I don't trust any migrant who tells me he's a professional. They can drive a taxi or a school bus. They can be landscapers or constructions workers. They can't even keep up a technical conversation with me."

"Would you trust me if I told you that during the nineties, I worked for four years as an Accounting Assistant Chief Section in the Pension Funds of a telecommunication company in Haiti (TELECO)?"

He sighs. "Ahh! You have to prove me."

"OK."

Let him live with his interrogations like many others do.

b) Hypocritical Conception

On my bus, during a trip to High School East, Dix Hills, one high school student asked another Haitian boy, "Are you Haitian?"

No answer.

"C'mon! I know you're Haitian."

He never answered.

Sincerely, that student is not alone. So many Haitian students suffer from this fear of identity. Clearly, it is a shame to hear my Haitians people talking negatively about their own country Haiti. Their comportment gives my mouth a bitter taste.

First, we do not exclude the fact that many parents decide not to visit Haiti for various reasons: bad faith, victim (or a close parent) of a scary experience, evasion following political persecutions, overwhelmed conscience, distraught with fear, fear of retaliation, insecurity, and so on...

Then many parents, stunned by the immensity of differences between the USA (the world's richest country) and Haiti (the poorest country in the hemisphere), do not have the courage or feel embarrassed to bring their children in the canton where they were born.

Finally, we can also say that that boy is a victim of a kind of fear orchestrated by our own peers. They let us understand that Haiti is "hell on earth." Many irresponsible Haitians swimming in the American ocean set themselves the dirty tasks of denigrating Haiti and, by way of consequence, making foreign people and even Haitians fear and stay away from this country named years ago "The Pearl of the Antilles."

Haitian migrants living in America have a choice to live either in Haiti or in the USA. Many of them say they have no family in Haiti. Lie! It would be a misfortune for Haitians to adopt the American family structure which is completely different from ours. We should not abandon this natural connection, this interrelation that exists between the complex Haitian family structure. What about the approximately ten millions who are living in Haiti? Most Haitians in the diaspora are tacitly contributing to the sinister destruction of their origin.

Since the earthquake of January 12, 2010, and even before, we face a sort of resentment of many Haitians and of other non-advised citizen of the world toward Haiti. This is a wrong, biased, and mean conception. Stop pushing us down! Please stop twisting the knife in the wounds. It hurts! Although Haiti is an *unsafe hell*, everyone still needs a piece.

Are we safe in this world? Tell me where. The world is rotten to the roots!

iv. The Cost of the Crossing

"I am a black, negro, Haitian, American, Caribbean" (Jean Price Mars) swimming in the American ocean, an environment where people of all races often smile to me. Is it a comic, ironic, affectionate, pitiful, cynical, hypocritical, or diplomatic smile? Or is it a manifestation of fear or a way to nip in the bud any bad intentions or any wrong preconceived ideas I might get in my mind? Or have they been told to have this attitude anytime they think a dangerous man is crossing their path? Sincerely, I do not bear any spirit of danger in me. Don't be scared; I am not a killer!

Like many others who bear an insatiable hunger for an ideal, I have left family members, friends, and a history behind. In pursuit of a sort of well-being, I have destroyed the original network I belonged to. We, as immigrant bus drivers, have been dispersed around the world. Some of us have been deviated from our way. Some of us swim around and learn to accommodate with other people who often offer us various sorts of hospitality.

What I have found? What are the costs of the crossing?

On the one hand, America, this school, is a great country that transforms our mentality, helps us understand differences, tolerate people's rudeness and madness, and cultivate incredible patience in our decisions, our actions, our behavior, etc. We, as school bus drivers, are doing a noble job that some Americans and, even some students, take a dim view of. In fact, in a store, I was talking to a mother whose daughter used to ride my bus every day to the middle school. Believe me, she despised her and said in front of me, "Mom, are you talking to Roman? He is a bus driver." I laughed because the mother is also a bus driver. Thanks, America, for preparing us to face those kinds of naïve judgments.

Depending on the content of our brain, our effort can help us move up through society and do challenging works that are allowed to the children of this nation. The American ocean can transform our ideal and shape us as a product we have never thought of. We can also reach the paroxysm of our dream and become a big fish depending on our position in the ocean. Our success can bring jealousy, contempt, and hatred of the unsuccessful fishes in the water. Or it can wrongly be seen or appreciated by the ones who are drowning.

On the other hand, so many families have been dislocated due to the exigencies of the immigration system. We will suffer the rest of our life after the death of a loved one. Some of us do not dare go to the funeral for fear of staying in our country. Remorse and unpleasant dreams are visible in our face. A heavy stone weighs forever on our stomach. Husbands, wives, children, etc., have broken their promises. Their pale faces reflect sadness. The system sometimes surrounds us everywhere. We have no bracelet, no chain, though we are not free to fly as a seagull. Victims of a kind of captivity, it gives us a feeling that nature is against us.

Therefore, depending on the circumstances, they would throw us to prison or set us free. Finally, whether we become free, or decide to be really free after retirement, the illusion of freedom will follow us like our shadow. In case of any chance, we will go back home to look in the face the ones we have despised, lowered, cursed, humiliated, dumped, lied to, betrayed, promised to, destroyed, exploited, yelled at, given false phone numbers to, hung up in their faces, and so on. At this time for sure, the burden of life will be too heavy for us, and our days will be counted until we tumble all the way down. Voila, that is all.

Voila, we are lost in an unknown environment where anytime we say a word, our stony accent puts our interlocutor in an embarrassing state and forces him to interrogate himself about our origin. Perhaps reading these lines, this pertinent question might come to your mind: "If it is so painful, why don't you go back to your country?"

Easy question; you are not the first one to raise such an interrogation.

I do not have an answer since the real answer would be beyond the spectrum of my understanding. But it is tangible that during the crossing, we have witnessed so many disappearances in the deep water of the ocean, though I am still swimming. Indeed, to swim is sometimes a fight against somebody stronger than us. Give me your hand, throw a cord at me, and pull me from the water. Please help me! It is too early to be drowned.

I do not have an answer, since the future doesn't belong to me. What belongs to me is to go step by step on an adventurous trip until I reach the destination.

The odds cannot tell me when I will reach the shore. But one thing remains evident: I do not "want to go through life without finding any satisfaction in the simple fact of being alive" (Jane O'Reilly, New York Magazine, Jan 17, 1972, p. 22). In other terms, who knows if the portion of time spent in the middle of the ocean is not the only time I will have? So I'd better make the most of it.

CHAPTER XXXI

The Last School Day

The last school day, I went down on Pulaski Road. I passed the jogger who was wearing a reflecting suit. Slowly, he was climbing and defying the slope with his strong legs. I did not pick up my Latino friend; the weather being nice, he probably decided to walk. While I was stopping for the red lights at the intersection of Pulaski and Larkfield Road, I glanced at the left to contemplate the East Northport Public Library. Since I have found this job, I frequented this library, which is located a few miles from the company.

To start that day, I did the morning route safely; and after having completed the high school and the middle school runs, I began the elementary school, the last run of the school day. The following lines are about it.

The last school day, a deafening noise reigned in the Forest Park Elementary School. That afternoon, nature offered one of its marvelous paintings. Many musical birds, multicolored butterflies, and insects of all kinds were frolicking in the infinite celestial sky. A quick look at the right parking lot let me observe many cautious parents who came to honor their commitments and to pick up their children at the school. All the caring and affectionate teachers and other curious onlookers were gathered on the sidewalk to greet the students for the last time. Indeed, they came out to liberate themselves, for a few months, from the burden of teaching and from its exigencies. Many teachers might also come out to get rid of some confusing situations they had faced throughout the school year.

Suddenly, one Half Hollow Hills School district bus driver blew its loud horn. Out of solidarity with him, other bus drivers responded. They gave an unpleasant and cacophonous concert that vibrated the students and other drivers' eardrums and broke the silence of the quiet and peaceful residential area in Dix Hills—a kind of warm-up that informed all the other bus drivers that it was about time to leave. For the last time that year, we, school bus drivers, started our buses and got ready to leave the school. The noise of the engines, the hot season, and the crowd of people gave place to an ambiance that reminded me of the St. Joseph Bus Station in Haiti, where Gran'n Tia, my great-grandmother, used to take my sister, Bobo, and me to summer vacation to Mirebalais, my family's hometown. In fact, for the last time that year, we felt the illusive happiness of completing the complex job of driving students.

Now, a teacher waved with her right hand to signal us to leave.

Let us tell you clearly and sincerely, in opposition to the rules, on that particular afternoon, students did not sit down right away on the bus. They all got up and stepped on the seats to enjoy this amazing event, to contemplate their dear teachers, to wave to them from the bus, to yell, to give their last wishes, their last kisses, or their last fingers. It would have been crazy to force them to sit down; this was one of their moments of euphoria that we could not control. Let them enjoy it, since it would only last for the space of a blinking.

So many will come back next year; many others will disappear for various other causes. All the children were standing; only Tristo, a little black boy, was sitting. With an ulcerous heart and a pale and wet face, he leaned his head against the window. Salted water of sadness, emptiness, pain, nostalgia, and regret flooded his face. I left my seat, came back in front of him, and kneeled. With my right hand on his small shoulder (I can feel his frail clavicle), I calmly asked him, "Why are you crying?"

"My teaacheeer," he answered.

"You'll be all right. You'll see her next year."

Probably it came into his mind, "It's vacation. I've to wait two months. I'm going to have another teacher in September." Perhaps he thought he just lost something he will never find again: a white female teacher's comprehension and tenderness. That afternoon, I saw that teacher stretch her arms to embrace and to show him the width of her love. His mother had a precarious health; she might not survive. The teacher was all for him, his only hope. Now she is gone, he was forced to go. He alone knew how immense his pain was. No possibility to measure it, but it was real and it weighed on the balance. Tristo was a troublemaker but a sensible, affectionate, and caring boy. He was a leader on my bus, and all the other students adored him and enjoyed his presence. For the last time, his teacher waved to him. Tears and mucus flooded his face; he was inconsolable, but it was time to leave.

While leaving the school, I held the steering wheel with the left hand; and with the right, with all my strength, I pushed down on the horn, playing then my partition in the concert. We followed the parade of the buses to Vanderbilt Parkway. Each bus driver went to his direction as a branch of a firework, each one with hundreds of stories, headed to his destination. When it was time to reinstate order inside, with my right hand, I invited my friends to sit down. I proceeded on and went up and down the different streets of Dix Hills.

For the last time, my students sang the lyrics: "Go, Roman, go. Go, Roman, go." For the last time that year, I danced for them. I hazardously danced for them swaying my head, my thorax, and my right wrist while the left hand held firmly the steering wheel. It was good to have some fun with them. It was good to break the apparent seriousness I feigned and made them feel good. Evidently, many of them laughed at my ungraceful moves. For that fraction of time, I liberated myself from various worries and obligations that the job and life required. Going down Bagatelle Road, I cautiously followed the curb and the dense clump of trees that gave me a feeling of home. Indeed, I thought I was strolling a path in the garden of Mirebalais like I was about to reach a river. And right away, a kind of nostalgia invaded me.

A look at the mirror showed me the change in my face and the students' faces. We have grown up and matured throughout the school year; others have reached the age of puberty. My face has also wrinkled due to the reflex movement of the muscles that protect my view against the reflections of sunlight and the glare of the oncoming cars. After dropping off all the children, and after post-tripping the bus, I headed back to the yard.

While driving throughout the school year, we have heard and seen so many things. We have heard things that leave painful memories, unpleasant things—things we did not want to hear and things that hurt and require years to be healed. We have also seen so many things under the sky, things that displeased us, things that left a sour taste in our mouth, and things that reduce us to the level of animality.

While going up Bagatelle Road, I looked again in the mirror; no one was behind me. I was the only one inside, as an island in the middle of the ocean. We have passed on average one hundred sixty days, twelve hundreds hours together, and I have driven them thousands of miles to destination. We have crossed towns, cities, and suburbs. I wanted to cry, since I might not see my troublemakers, my headaches, my "calculus book," my problems; I might never see my innocent passengers, my friends, my jokers, and my close bodyguards anymore. Now, I understood that the school year was really over.

I headed back to the Expressway, the flow of the cars passed me every few seconds. You would say that I was not moving. No one wanted to stay behind me. I passed a car that was doing less than fifty-five miles per hour; to retaliate the driver sped up and dangerously cut me off. The back of her car almost touched me like the tail of an angry snake that wanted to whip me for I just disturbed her lethargic sleep. I released the brake pedal, giving her more room. "It is the last school day, babe. No more accident! No more drug test!" I murmured.

The drivers hate the school bus. It is too big, too slow, and too lazy; in fact, it is the patient turtle that will surely reach the destination. It sometimes follows the regulations and forces other vehicles to comply with the rules. I headed back to the Kings Park Yard, with bus 30153 remained intact: no broken gauges, mirrors, and windows; no scratches; no breakdown. Thank God!

I managed to stay vigilant and protect the exploited landscaper; the strong jogger; the widower walking her dog; the teenager wearing a headset, texting, and flying into space; the undecided animal; and so on. Thousands of times, I checked my seven mirrors, drawing clockwise with my head the pentagon, my symbol of prevention. I breathed deeply to exhale the ups and downs of the job and all its complexity, the problems encountered with rude students, with other drivers, with parents, and with employees, etc. We, as school bus drivers and any other drivers who have to sit down long hours, know how painful and sensitive our backs are after a trip; we know how painful and lame our first steps are before we regain our cadence after our knee joints have become lubricated; and we know how difficult it is to read the mileage gauge after a whole day driving.

We sometimes find it difficult to liberate us from some states of remorse that have followed us a certain time—remorse for having yelled at the wrong child, or for having reported the wrong student; remorse for having prevented, too late, a bully whose traumatic consequences are already disastrous to the victim; remorse for having been biased with the American teenager; remorse for wrongly cutting off a car, a truck in the streets, or for having talked rudely on the two-way radio to a dispatcher or a manager; and so on.

We are also conscious, aren't we, that other challenges are waiting for us next year. Oftentimes, as we know, the spirit of lucre, the instinct of survival, the insatiable character of human being, the search of happiness and well-being have forced many drivers to fight even on their knees for what belongs to them. We know how the new, rational, and tough management system has apparently kept us, drivers, away from the chain as a broken link, although in reality we are not. We know how evident is the politic of discouragement of some senior drivers to the benefit of some new drivers: the latter used to work more hours. It is a simple and preliminary arithmetic calculation, whose objective is to maximize the company's profit. Furthermore, we know how the conflict of interest, how the confrontation of egoism, how the principles created by the improvised laws of some dispatchers or managers to regulate us, have dampened the ambiance of family that existed before and have precipitated, at its paroxysm, an antecedent: the necessity of the birth of a union.

Finally, it is the completion of a long school year. I clear myself for not having caused too many hazardous stupidities and for having prevented other drivers' rudeness that could lead to a disaster. With a clear conscience, I headed back, cleared of all the job's requirements and responsibilities. Goodbye, the funny smell of the dump trucks! Goodbye, cold sweat and palpitations when I am lost! Behind my seat is a bag full of envelopes. For sure, inside them are not only greeting cards with words that come from the parents and children's hearts but also with money. I mean real money. With a last look at the mirror, I saw my face. I wiped it with the right hand. I said to myself, "Is it you, Roman?"

"Yeah! It's me."

It is me with the sword of Damocles hanged on top of my head. It did not fall that year; it does not fall yet, but it has swung on many occasions. At least, I have read all the problems in the "calculus book," but I still have not solved all of them. My assigned task as a school bus driver is apparently completed. Am I done? Probably yes for the regular school year, but not for the whole year. Yes, it is an end, but not the end. Or more precisely, it is "the end of a beginning" (Sir Winston Churchill Speech, Nov. 1942), since we are spinning in a cycle without an exit.

Can we take vacation? Question of choice.

I entered the company yard, post-tripped the bus for the last time. Opening both arms and yawning at the same time, I stretched all my body; and while I was closing my eyes, I cried, "Ayyyyy Manman! It's over." I took the bag of envelopes, walked back to the office, and handed the key and the paperwork to the dispatcher. I got in my car and left the yard to go home. I left with my disappointments, my regrets, my smile, my souvenirs, as all students, parents, friends, coworkers have left with theirs. Each one of us left to his misery, to his own destiny, or to his success.

For many circumstances, some will disappear during the summer. One day will be my turn, though the work and my mission to the students still go on and should continue.

When I got home, tired after a full year of work, I took a warm shower, did the sign of the cross three times, and went to sleep through the night with my alarms off, since I did not have to wake up early tomorrow.

www.ingramcontent.com/pod-product-compliance
Lightning Source LLC
Chambersburg PA
CBHW021619120626
46545CB00001B/308